AMERICAN THEATRE
BOOK OF MONOLOGUES
FOR MEN

AMERICAN THEATRE BOOK OF MONOLOGUES FOR MEN

EDITED BY STEPHANIE COEN

THEATRE COMMUNICATIONS GROUP
NEW YORK
2003

American Theatre Book of Monologues for Men is published by Theatre Communications Group, Inc., 520 Eighth Ave., 24th Floor, New York, NY 10018-4156

This publication is made possible in part with funds from the New York State Council on the Arts, a State Agency.

TCG books are exclusively distributed to the book trade by Consortium Book Sales and Distribution, 1045 Westgate Dr., St. Paul, MN 55114.

LIBRARY OF CONGRESS CATALOGING-IN-PUBLICATION DATA
American theatre book of monologues for men / edited by Stephanie Coen.
—1st ed.
p. cm.
Audition monologues selected from plays first published in American theatre magazine since 1985.
ISBN 1-55936-197-2 (pbk. : alk. paper)
1. Monologues. 2. Acting—Auditions. 3. American drama—20th century.
4. Men—Drama. I. Coen, Stephanie. II. American theatre magazine.

PN2080.A478 2001
812'.045089286—dc21   2001027315

Cover design by Carin Goldberg
Book design and composition by Lisa Govan

First Edition, August 2003

ACKNOWLEDGMENTS

I am grateful to Todd London, editor of TCG's previous volumes of *Contemporary American Monologues*, in whose footsteps I have happily followed for many years. I owe a great deal to TCG's exemplary publications department, particularly Terry Nemeth for the opportunity, Kathy Sova for her judicious editing, and Todd Miller and Gretchen Van Lente for their able assistance.

Thanks also to my bosses, present and past: Bartlett Sher, artistic director of Intiman Theatre; Jim O'Quinn, editor of *American Theatre* magazine; and the three leaders of the field whom I was lucky enough to work for during my seven years at TCG: Ben Cameron, Lindy Zesch and, especially, Peter Zeisler, who taught me more than he might know, and whose lessons I still value.

I owe a special debt to all of the playwrights whose work is included in this volume for their talent and generosity, and for allowing us to include excerpts from their plays, in some instances cobbled together to make sense out of context. Where lines of dialogue or stage directions have been cut, a bracketed ellipsis [...] marks the deletion.

For my parents,
and for Yohanan, Avigail
and Elinoam Ben-Gad

CONTENTS

INTRODUCTION

In the November 1985 issue of *American Theatre*, critic James Leverett introduced the first play published in the magazine, Emily Mann's *Execution of Justice*, with these words: "This month *American Theatre* begins what we all hope will be a long, distinguished career of play publication with a work that is not supposed to exist: a play by a contemporary American author concerning events and issues of historical scope and import."

Very nearly two decades and (as of July 2003) 100 scripts later, *American Theatre*'s record of play publication is, indeed, long and distinguished. The monologues included in this volume were all culled from texts that were published, often for the first time and always in their entirety, in the magazine. Whether or not all of these plays reflect "historical scope and import" is, of course, a matter of debate. What remains indisputable is that they are, together, a record of the contemporary American theatre, of what our playwrights were thinking and writing about as the millennium approached (to borrow a phrase) and the new century began.

From the first issue, the magazine's mandate was, in part, to select plays that had already been produced in a number of theatres. There was no directive to "discover"—or hype—the latest talent. By seeking out new plays that were being produced throughout the country, however, the magazine helped bring adventurous, provocative and original writers to greater public attention and critical acclaim, often with their earliest works. Before the first decade passed, *American Theatre* had published Eric Bogosian, Constance Congdon, Christopher Durang, Maria Irene Fornes, Craig Lucas and George C. Wolfe, to name only a half-dozen of an impressive assemblage. In later years, Edward Albee, Steven Dietz, Tony Kushner, Donald Margulies, Suzan-Lori Parks, Sam Shepard, Octavio Solis, Paula Vogel, Naomi Wallace—and so many others—would join them.

These writers and the others published by *American Theatre* (and in Theatre Communications Group's book program) are of different generations and disparate backgrounds, with shared influences but idiosyncratic styles and sensibilities. Their plays take many forms and are many things—wild riffs on history, absurdist comedies and dramatic reveries, elegies for loss, explorations of the families we are born into (usually dysfunctional) and the families we create, and fierce mediations on what it has meant to be "other" in America. They range from the personal to the political to the poetic (although some are both political and poetic simultaneously), with excursions into farce, autobiography and, of course, the well-made play.

The structure of this book is borrowed from TCG's previously published volumes of monologues, *Contemporary American Monologues for Men* and *Contemporary American Monologues for Women*, both of which were edited by the astute and inimitable Todd London. As in the earlier collections, the monologues are grouped in named chapters by themes and connections, rather than broken down according to the actor's age range or the style of the work. Relevant information about the character and other necessary background about the play is included in the introductory paragraph to each piece. A glance at the chapter headings should give you a quick sense of the emotional tenor or subject matter of the works that will follow.

For the actor, the intention of this volume is to provide strong material for use in auditions or acting classes. As excerpted, the monologues are meant to be resonant pieces independent of their original dramatic context, but I encourage you, more than anything else, to read the plays from which they are extracted—the best and truest way to uncover their full potential and understand your character. (Publication information is included at the back of this book, in the Further Reading section.)

As a collection, these plays are a testament to TCG, and *American Theatre*'s, commitment to the enduring ambitions of contemporary playwriting. "Make sure if you're trying to impress me with the depth and complexity of your work that you've got material to match it," director Bartlett Sher says in the interview that follows. "If you want your work to be rich and interesting, the monologue needs to be rich and interesting." These selections reflect some of the best and most surprising voices in the contemporary theatre. Now it is for you, as an actor, to bring these pieces to life, and by so doing, fully explore and inhabit the worlds that they evoke.

—S.C.

BE SPECIFIC: THE ACTOR'S APPROACH TO THE MONOLOGUE

An Interview with Bartlett Sher, Artistic Director, Intiman Theatre, Seattle

What should an actor look for in choosing audition material?
I always answer this question based on my own instinct, not from what's going to get an actor a job. Never pick something you wrote. It's a terrible idea, not because you might not be a good writer, but because I can't evaluate it honestly. I want you to be there to act, and interpret something you didn't write.

It's important to pick something that is right for you, in the obvious sense that it would be a part you would be good at playing. If you have played a part—and played it well, and were really guided in it—I would use it. That's more important than showing versatility. The monologue should also be close to the part for which you're auditioning. Many things are being evaluated: speech and voice work, to some extent physical skills, and being able to play through a clear single action in the course of the monologue.

If I'm auditioning for a Shakespeare play, even a small part, and all I have is the monologue to go on, I want to see that the person is so good at the monologue, so close to the character, that I might find them useful for other parts in the play. If I'm auditioning for *Richard II*, I'm not going to cast

Richard out of a general monologue audition, but I might learn that I could find a Bushy, a Bagot or a Green. You need to pick a monologue that shows how good an artist you are *and* how valuable you will be in the other parts. I've often become interested in people who are great with verse, who are funny, who are pure and clear and still and strong.

What makes a good audition monologue?

It's important that you are playing a single action, and that I watch you playing an action. Actors will often try to illustrate everything that is going on in the whole play—so I never see the actual acting, I see all the results. They will do, for instance, Edmund's speech from *King Lear* about being a bastard, and they will show what a terribly bad person they are. But that speech is also about Edmund coming to a conclusion and working his way through a problem. All Shakespeare monologues come in three parts—a beginning, middle and an end—and the revelation of the speeches is always about what the character is trying to do or work out.

Actors need to get the focus on what their character is trying to accomplish, instead of on the character itself. People tend to do monologues alone and take out the other characters in the scene. But even if it's a Shakespeare soliloquy and you are alone, there is always interaction. Always be very specific about who the audience is to the character at that moment—are they a best friend, are they a confidant, etc. When they are not just "the audience," you can play the action and be in the scene more completely. Otherwise you may just be performing, as opposed to acting.

What about working with a monologue from the contemporary theatre?

It's always appropriate to stay within the genre you're working. If you are auditioning for a comedy, make the monologue a comedy; if it's a tragedy, make it a tragedy. In a general audition, your common sense will tell you what you're good at. I always like simplicity and purity, as opposed to using the monologue to "feel" something. That's always the worst. If somebody comes in and they're crying by the end of the monologue, that's a nightmare.

Actors should approach contemporary writers with the same level of care and scoring and attention to language and rhythm that they do Shakespeare. If it's David Mamet or John Guare or Arthur Miller or Harold Pinter, there's usually an internal rhythm, and a real choice of language, that reveals potent and profound information over the course of the monologue. Often people will get relaxed in the language and become more concerned about the "performance"; yet the language has all the real information in it.

When an actor walks into an audition, what are you looking for?
I usually audition intensively—like a diagnostic test. I will take the actor through a series of choices and see what they can pull off. I won't necessarily have in my head a set thing. Obviously, there are things that the part requires, and there are things that the person brings to the part, in terms of intelligence and heart. Those are the two critical things—mind and heart.

If the audition is conducted without a monologue, and it usually is, I'm testing for whether or not I'm going to have a good collaborator. So I will ask questions to see what kind of responses I get, to gauge the actor's level of thinking. If it's an audition with a monologue, what usually happens is that people try to use the monologue to show *all* the things they can do well. They will illustrate every line, emotionally, physically or verbally. They will pack it with all the things that they are good at. So now it's not an experience of a monologue in time, it's an experience of a résumé in the form of a monologue. But it's more important that an actor make one choice (or a few strong choices) and hold with that, rather than make too many choices.

How does it affect you, as the caster/director, if you know the work, and you are aware of the context of the monologue within the play?

That's hard, because you get into a region where my supposedly intelligent opinion intersects with your choices. What hopefully *won't* happen is that I think I'm so smart that I'm just going to tell you how to do it. If you did the monologue really well and I thought you were really on it and it looked like you could do it—that is, be in the play, in that part—I will have discovered that you have some chops. I won't learn anything if you are using it to do anything else, like break down and cry.

What are the pitfalls of an audition—what should an actor avoid?

As I said, anything you wrote yourself. Anything personal—don't believe *in* anything, play a character. People often turn monologues into testimonies; acting is not about telling me something you feel about the world. Otherwise it's *Oprah*. I need to see characters that don't know what they believe in because they're in the middle of it.

Don't pick material that's too mundane, because sometimes your work will be better than the material. And you can never beat the material—the material will always win. So make sure if you're trying to impress me with the depth and complexity of your work that you've got material to match it. If you want your work to be rich and interesting, the monologue needs to be rich and interesting.

Anything narrative is really bad—if it's narrative, you're not playing anything, you're telling me a story. The character has got to be somebody in the middle of circumstances, playing an action on somebody else. If there is a clear facility for language, if you are clearly playing to or against another person, if your work is clearly fresh and on the thoughts, I am going to listen better. If I'm seeing you be a character in specific circumstances, then I'm wondering what's going to happen by the end of the monologue. That's all a monologue has to do.

Let's talk about humor in an audition—how hard is it to be funny?

It's not that hard—if you are a funny person. It's not easy to do in the case of creating funny voices and goofy walks. That's a different kind of funny. Usually humor is about being deep in the circumstances, and about reaching some level of pain, panic and agony, which leads to those circumstances getting out of control. If it's really active, then it's funny. When it isn't active, then it isn't funny.

We all have seen a lot of date plays, love plays, relationships plays—and usually it's the pain of failure that makes the joke. Irony and sarcasm are really hard to pull off, because they are a little bit too smart.

What about an actor's physicality?

I'm exceptionally attuned to physicality, to relaxation and a quiet body, as opposed to a frenzied one. If a physical choice is made, it's got to be extremely precise. I have no set rules, like more physical or less physical; you just have to be very good at whatever you choose to do, and very clear and specific. As an audition goes on I'll bust anybody whose body is not behaving, or is not really connected. In the silhouette of a character, in the physical signature of a character, is an enormous amount of information. If somebody makes a strong physical choice, and they pull it off, it can be extremely revealing and extremely impressive.

How do you work with the actor in the audition?

If an actor has laid down a good path in a monologue, I'll then give them choices to play with to see if I can push them somewhere, and that then becomes a small model of what rehearsal will be like—are they versatile, do they get the idea, do they understand what I'm talking about, do they have the chops to implement something? I'll take them through a lot of colors, line to line to line to line, to see if they have versatility and to keep them on track of the action. It's at this time that I start to find out if somebody has a propensity for working with me or not.

They don't have to do what I'm looking for, but they have to do something interesting that's going to take the material somewhere new that neither of us might have expected. That's when you begin to see a possible collaborator—they listen really well; they respond in an interesting and creative way; they take the work somewhere that is either exactly what I had in mind and reveals it fully, or somewhere completely different that amazes us both. I don't like people who enter the profession because they were talented and have a series of tricks at their disposal. That's not as interesting to me as having real collaborators who have their own ideas.

Are the rules different when you're working with a student in a classroom situation?

The rules are never different. There may be different levels of skill, but the rules of what it takes to make the work good are never different. What makes a person rich and interesting in their work is probably not known, even to that person. It's just a lot of practice and a lot of talent—and talent is the most mysterious thing. What is one person's talent versus another's is unknown, but it's either there or not there. It either plays loud and big in them or it is small and tiny, and you can't tell why.

Do actors have "types"?

I prefer to cast against type, but sometimes type is type. I've worked in a lot of companies where we frequently had to cast against type, and it would almost always have good results, especially in a play that people knew; it subverted the audiences' expectations and allowed the play to be something fresh. But there are certain types that must be obeyed, and therefore you really have to get somebody who is right inside of that. Not every person in a show can be cast against type.

Actors hate type because it makes them feel that they are categorized, and I don't blame them. It's the hardest thing in the world to find two great ingénues, because all actors want to be character actors: they all want to be something else. Getting somebody who is really good at being an ingénue— surprising and rich and attractive and fun—is harder than finding a good character actor.

What would your advice be when an actor comes in for an audition—play to type or against it?
It depends on what they want. If they are good at their type, know they're good at their type and want to tell me that they're good at their type, that's what they should do. If they have versatility, or if they believe they can really nail an ingénue and also play one of the clowns, they should do both.

If you know yourself, and are connected to what you can do well, then you should show me. If you don't know yourself and are not connected, you're going to try to show me something that you don't really feel close to, and I'm not going to get it. Or, if I do, it will be a false representation of who you are anyway. Some people are great rock stars and bad actors. Some great actors can convince me they're rock stars. As an actor, it's the hardest thing in the world to learn who you are, and accept who you are, and then be able to play with and mold that. There are different kinds of actors; the ones who do one kind of thing really well, and those who do many things well.

How might these personal qualities that you're talking about manifest themselves in an audition?
Some people tend to believe that their personality will be so fun and engaging that no one will be able to resist their charm when it comes to the audition. Often it is the reverse: it can make me really annoyed, because I like the personality to be displayed in the work.

Lots of actors get taught to be very obedient, and that's not it either. If you get asked a lot of questions, don't just slavishly obey and try to make the person who is holding the audition happy. Actors are always afraid they are going to be rejected—that's all over them—they torture themselves, and then there's too much neediness in the interaction that leads to the audition. Be yourself, and be professional. Put your work out there and then let it go. You might be right for the part, you might not.

One last question—do you have a favorite monologue?
I don't, but I have some that I've heard an awful lot. In the Shakespeare world, there's a couple that you hear all the time. I've been in the middle of productions where I've thought, This would make such a great monologue, how come I've never heard it? Usually it's because the monologue only has a single thought in it, and people then don't do it. There's Posthumus' monologue in *Cymbeline*, for instance, where he rails against women. It's a hateful, evil monologue that's just as interesting as Edmund's bastard speech in *King Lear*, which I've heard one billion times. I always like to be surprised, and I like to be reassured.

"Surprised and reassured"—what do you mean by that?
If somebody's doing two monologues, you want to know that they are really good at what they do, and then you want to be surprised. Sometimes both happen at the same time, but not always. Monologue auditioning is difficult because it's sort of lateral to what the work is going to be—it's only a way of introducing yourself, not a way of finally getting the part. As a way of introducing yourself, it's best to choose a monologue that reflects what's extremely wonderful about you.

Bartlett Sher is artistic director of Intiman Theatre in Seattle, Washington, where his credits include the commissioned world premiere of *Nickel and Dimed*, a play written by Joan Holden and based on the book by Barbara Ehrenreich, which debuted as part of Intiman's thirtieth anniversary season in 2002. He made his Seattle directing debut in 2001 with Shakespeare's *Cymbeline* and directed a new production of the play for Theatre for a New Audience, which premiered in England at the Royal Shakespeare Company with an American cast, and had an award-winning Off-Broadway run in New York. For the New York production, he received the 2002 Joe A. Callaway Award from the Stage Directors and Choreographers Foundation. His additional credits include Molière's *Don Juan* and the American premiere of Harley Granville Barker's 1907 play *Waste* (2000 OBIE Award for Best Play), both produced by Theatre for a New Audience. Prior to coming to Intiman in 2000, he served as associate artistic director at Hartford Stage Company, company director at the Guthrie Theater and associate artist at the Idaho Shakespeare Festival. He has taught and run workshops throughout his career in the United States and internationally.

1

"WE WERE A WELL-ESTABLISHED FAMILY ONCE."

BURIED CHILD

By Sam Shepard

This Pulitzer Prize–winning play is a gothic, dysfunctional-family comic tragedy. Shepard's 1996 revision of his 1978 play emphasizes the play's humor, particularly in the character of Dodge, a man in his seventies who has killed a child—the "buried child" of his wife and their son, Tilden. "I think the play works because the audience is allowed into this kind of strange humor in spite of themselves," Shepard said in an American Theatre *magazine interview. "They have to laugh at this character, even though he's killed a child. Otherwise, it's deadly." In this speech, Dodge breaks the family pact to reveal their long-withheld secret. He addresses the speech to Shelly, his grandson's girlfriend, but speaks also to the reluctant Halie, forcing her to listen.*

DODGE: See, we were a well-established family once. Well-established. All the boys were grown. The farm was producing enough milk to fill Lake Michigan twice over. Me and Halie here were pointed toward what looks like the middle part of our life. Everything was settled with us. All we had to do was ride it out. Then Halie got pregnant again. Out the middle a nowhere, she got pregnant. We weren't planning on havin' any more boys. We had enough boys already. In fact, we hadn't been sleepin' in the same bed for about six years. [. . .]
    Halie had this kid see. This baby boy. She had it. I let her have it on her own. All the other boys I had had the best doc-

tors, the best nurses, everything. This one I let her have by herself. This one hurt real bad. Almost killed her, but she had it anyway. It lived, see. It lived. It wanted to grow up in this family. It wanted to be just like us. It wanted to be part of us. It wanted to pretend that I was its father. She wanted me to believe in it. Even when everyone around us knew. Everyone. All our boys knew. Tilden knew. [. . .] Tilden was the one who knew. Better than any of us. He'd walk for miles with that kid in his arms. Halie let him take it. All night sometimes. He'd walk all night out there in the pasture with it. Talkin' to it. Singin' to it. Used to hear him singing to it. He'd make up stories. He'd tell that kid all kinds a stories. Even when he knew it couldn't understand him. We couldn't let a thing like that continue. We couldn't allow that to grow up right in the middle of our lives. It made everything we'd accomplished look like it was nothin'. Everything was canceled out by this one mistake. This one weakness. [. . .]

I killed it. I drowned it. Just like the runt of a litter. Just drowned it. There was no struggle. No noise. Life just left it.

BURIED CHILD

By Sam Shepard

Twenty-two-year-old Vince has arrived unannounced at the home of his grandparents, Dodge and Halie, after six years of separation. But when he gets there, no one knows who he his. Vince's search for self-knowledge and recognition is the heart of Shepard's 1996 revision of his Pulitzer Prize–winning play, which originally premiered in 1978. At the end of the play, Vince disappears in the middle of the night to buy liquor with two dollars given to him by his grandfather. He returns the next morning drunk and exhausted. Here, he tells his girl-

friend Shelly where he has been, but delivers the speech out front, Shepard says, to the audience. At the end of the speech, Shelly will leave him.

VINCE: I was gonna run last night. I was gonna run and keep right on running. Clear to the Iowa border. I drove all night with the windows open. The old man's two bucks flapping right on the seat beside me. It never stopped raining the whole time. Never stopped once. I could see myself in the windshield. My face. My eyes. I studied my face. Studied everything about it as though I was looking at another man. As though I could see his whole race behind him. Like a mummy's face. I saw him dead and alive at the same time. In the same breath. In the windshield I watched him breathe as though he was frozen in time and every breath marked him. Marked him forever without him knowing. And then his face changed. His face became his father's face. Same bones. Same eyes. Same nose. Same breath. And his father's face changed to his grandfather's face. And it went on like that. Changing/ Clear on back to faces I'd never seen before but still recognized. Still recognized the bones underneath. Same eyes. Same mouth. Same breath. I followed my family clear into Iowa. Every last one. Straight into the corn belt and further. Straight back as far as they'd take me. Then it all dissolved/ Everything dissolved. Just like that. And that two bucks kept right on flapping on the seat beside me.

THREE DAYS OF RAIN

By Richard Greenberg

Walker Janeway, his childhood friend Pip says, is capable of changing "the temperature of every circumstance by [a] kind of tyrannical psychosocial, you know, fiat." A year after he disap-

peared to Italy without a word to his sister Nan or his friends,
Walker has returned to Manhattan for the reading of his late father's
will. He addresses the audience in the first speech of the play.

WALKER: My name is Walker Janeway. I'm the son of Edmund
Janeway, whose slightly premature death caused such a stir
last year, I'm told. As you're probably aware, my father, along
with that tribe of acolytes who continue to people the firm of
Wexler Janeway, designed all—yes, all—of the most famous
buildings of the last thirty years. You've seen their pictures, you
may have even visited a few. That Shi'ite mosque in Idaho. The
new library in Burges. The crafts museum in Austin, that hos-
pice I forget where, and a vertical mall in Rhode Island that in
square footage actually exceeds the *state* of Rhode Island.

Years and years and years ago, with his late partner,
Theodore Wexler, my father also designed three or four buildings that truly *are* distinguished, chief among them: Janeway
House. I know you know that one. Everyone's seen that one picture, *LIFE Magazine*, April of '63, I think, where it looks lunar,
I mean, like something carved from the moon, mirage-y—you
remember that photo? It's beautiful, isn't it? It won some kind
of non–Pulitzer Prize that year. People have sometimes
declined my invitation to see the real place for fear of ruining
the experience of the photograph.

Well. The real place, as it happens, is a private home out
in the desirable part of Long Island. My grandparents commissioned it of my father, using all the money they had in the
world, because, I guess, they loved him so much. Apparently,
there was something there for a parent to love. Hard to imagine how they could tell, though, since he seldom actually
spoke. Maybe he was lovable in a Chaplinesque way. Whatever, their faith paid off. The house is deemed, by those who
matter, to be one of the great private residences of the last half-
century.

It's empty now.

My sister and I will inherit it today.

We'll be the only family present. Unless you count our friend, Pip, who is my late father's late partner's torpid son.

My mother would be, as well, of course, but she's um, like, well, she's sort of like Zelda Fitzgerald's less stable sister, so she can't be there. She's somewhere else, she's . . .

So, then, this is the story as I know it so far: my father was more-or-less silent; my mother was more-or-less mad. They married because by 1960 they had reached a certain age and they were the last ones left in the room.

And then they had my sister who is somehow *entirely* sane.

And then they had me.

And my father became spectacularly successful, and his partner died shockingly young, and my mother grew increasingly mad, and my sister and I were there so we had to grow up.

And today we receive our legacy.

2

"IT WAS LOVE. ALWAYS LOVE."

A QUESTION OF MERCY

By David Rabe

David Rabe's play was inspired by Dr. Richard Selzer's New York Times Magazine *essay about his personal experience with the issue of assisted suicide.*

Anthony—stricken with AIDS and in terrible, constant pain—decides to end his own life. He enlists the support of his lover Thomas and a sympathetic doctor. Trying to convince his doctor to help him, Anthony tells him about what it was like to grow up gay in his native Colombia (where "one is better off not to be a homosexual, or at least not to know if they are") and how his life changed when he met Thomas.

ANTHONY: These feelings piercing my childhood, this undeniable attraction to men. It was not so much my self changing. It was more exactly my understanding that changed. A strange blooming in a field of perfect ignorance. I struggled, of course, with the common confusions. Though they scarcely mattered, because it was impossible to express it, these feelings, even if I had understood them fully. Even much later, at the university in Bogotá where I went to study, and where I lived for six years, in an apartment with six other male students, I did not express it. It was a quiet student life. We were friends, that's all. Then I came to New York, lived in freedom. [. . .] I traveled here to attend NYU. That's when I met him and fell in love with him. This was in 1980. When my studies were complete we separated for two years, as people do when they misunderstand the deepest design of their lives. But we had the wisdom to stay in contact. Those two years ended, as if they had been imposed and we began to live together. When I felt ill, it was just an infection, I was certain, though I worried about AIDS. I told Thomas at once, and we agreed that we must discontinue sex and so we did. From that day forward, aside from mutual caressing, there has been no sexual contact between us. And this has had its difficulties of course, but they have been of surprisingly little consequence, because, as it turns out, it was not sex that mattered so much between us ever anyway—not really—it was not sex that kept us together, or brought us together in the first place. It was love. Always love.

IN THE BLOOD

By Suzan-Lori Parks

Suzan-Lori Parks gives each of the adult characters in her modern-day riff on The Scarlet Letter *"confessions," interior monologues that are shared with the audience. A dramatic device for the characters to reveal events that happened off-stage, or in the past, the confessions give a dramatic context to the seemingly good and upright citizens who exploit Hester, La Negrita and her five illegitimate children. While the word "confessions" implies an unburdening, a revelation of some wrongdoing, these monologues are delivered without apology or shame.*

Chilli and Hester had a love affair once—a romance that ended when Chilli, "infatuated" with drugs, abandoned Hester when she was pregnant. Now, fourteen years later, he returns to see her, a changed man—only to leave her again when he discovers that she has five illegitimate children (see Chilli's monologue later in the volume). Chilli remembers

what it was like when they were young and in love in this con-
fession, delivered moments after he first proposes marriage.

Note: the "(Rest)," an aspect of what Parks understat-
edly calls her use of "slightly unconventional theatrical ele-
ments," signifies "a little time, a pause, a breather," a transi-
tion for the actor and the character.

CHILLI:
We was young
and we didnt think
we didnt think that nothing we could do would hurt us
nothing we did would come back to haunt us
we was young and we knew all about gravity but gravity
    was a law that did not apply to those persons under
    the age of 18
gravity was something that came later
and we was young and we could
float
weightless
I was her first
and zoom to the moon if we wanted and couldnt nothing
    stop us
we could go
fast
and we were gonna live forever
and any mistakes we would shake off
we were Death Defying
we were Hot Lunatics
careless as all get out
and she needed to keep it and I needed to leave town.
People get old that way.
(Rest)
We didnt have a car and everything was pitched
    toward love in a car
and there was this car lot down from where we worked
    and

we were fearless
late nights go sneak in those rusted Buicks that hadnt
    moved in years
I would sit at the wheel and pretend to drive
and she would say she felt the wind in her face
surfing her hand out the window
then we'd park
without even moving
in the full light of the lot
making love—
She was my first.
We was young.
Times change.

IN THE HEART OF AMERICA

By Naomi Wallace

In the Heart of America *is a fierce indictment of homophobia
and racism in the U.S. military. Fairouz, a young Palestinian-
American woman, is trying to discover what really happened
to her brother Remzi, who died during the Gulf War. She seeks
out his friend Craver Perry, also a soldier, who comes from a
lower-class family in Kentucky. Craver finally reveals that
Remzi was his lover, and that he was killed after being gay-
bashed by other soldiers. Craver is with Fairouz but speaks
directly to Remzi, who has appeared as a vision.*

CRAVER: The first time we made love, we were so scared and
I started to cry. It was a first time for both of us and it hurt.
You leaned over me and kissed the back of my neck and you
said over and over: You are my white trash and I love you.
They caught us together, out behind the barracks. They were
lower ranks. Just kids. Like me. Kids who grew up with

garbage in their backyards. Kids who never got the summer jobs, who didn't own CD players. They knocked us around. After a while, they took us to a room. Handed us over to an upper rank. There was a British officer and an Iraqi prisoner in there too and they were laughing and saying: sandnigger. Indian. Gook. *(Beat)* Remzi. Well. He went wild. He jumped one of those officers. I was standing there. I couldn't move. I couldn't . . . Then somebody hit me over the head and I went out. *(Beat)* The first time I came to, the prisoner was down and he kept waving his arms like he was swimming, doing the backstroke, and Remzi was there and I could hear his voice but it was like trying to see through a sheet of ice. *(Beat)* My head was spinning and it was snowing stars. In that room. In the middle of the biggest bunch of hottest nowhere in the world and it was snowing stars and Remzi in the center of it and this one officer or maybe it was two and there was a knife and the Iraqi had stopped moving—I think he was dead—and they were all over him and having a good time at it. Like kids in the snow. *(Beat)* Do you want to know how you died, Remzi? [. . .] One of them had his arm around my neck, choking me, while another one held you down. I shouted for you to stay down but you wouldn't stay down. Each time he knocked you down you stood up. He hit you in the mouth so many times I couldn't tell anymore what was your nose and what was your mouth. *(Beat)* [. . .] When I woke up, I took him in my arms. The blood had stopped coming out. *(Beat)* Five foot . . . eleven inches. That's how tall you were. I used to run my hands up and down your body like I was reading the bones.

M. BUTTERFLY

By David Henry Hwang

Suggested by real-life events, David Henry Hwang's Tony Award–winning play tells the story of Rene Gallimard, a French diplomat who fell in love with a Chinese opera singer. After a relationship that lasted twenty years, Gallimard discovered that his "mistress" was actually a man and a Communist spy. Hwang's investigation into the sexual and emotional ambiguity of their union is a gender-bending take on Puccini's Madame Butterfly, *Gallimard's favorite opera.*

The play takes the form of a long confession, with Gallimard addressing the audience from prison, where the now-disgraced diplomat has been sentenced for his own (inadvertent) Vietnam-era espionage. During this final monologue he dons a wig and kimono, becoming the true Butterfly—not the "feminine ideal, beautiful and brave" that he always saw in Puccini's opera, but the betrayed lover who will, at the end of the speech, plunge a knife into his own body.

GALLIMARD: I've played out the events of my life night after night, always searching for a new ending to my story, one where I leave this cell and return forever to my Butterfly's arms.

Tonight I realize my search is over. That I've looked all along in the wrong place. And now, to you, I will prove that my love was not in vain—by returning to the world of fantasy where I first met her.

There is a vision of the Orient that I have. Of slender women in chong sams and kimonos who die for the love of unworthy foreign devils. Who are born and raised to be the perfect women. Who take whatever punishment we give them, and bounce back, strengthened by love, unconditionally. It is a vision that has become my life.

In public, I have continued to deny that Song Liling is a man. This brings me headlines, and is a source of great embarrassment to my French colleagues, who can now be sent into a coughing fit by the mere mention of Chinese food. But alone, in my cell, I have long since faced the truth. And the truth demands a sacrifice. For mistakes made over the course of a lifetime. My mistakes were simple and absolute—the man I loved was a cad, a bounder. He deserved nothing but a kick in the behind, and instead I gave him . . . all my love. Yes— love. Why not admit it all? That was my undoing, wasn't it? Love warped my judgment, blinded my eyes, rearranged the very lines on my face . . . until I could look in the mirror and see nothing but . . . a woman.

I have a vision. Of the Orient. That, deep within its almond eyes, there are still women. Women willing to sacrifice themselves for the love of a man. Even a man whose love is completely without worth.

Death with honor is better than life . . . life with dishonor. The love of a Butterfly can withstand many things— unfaithfulness, loss, even abandonment. But how can it face the one sin that implies all others? The devastating knowledge that, underneath it all, the object of her love was nothing more, nothing less than . . . a man. It is 1988. And I have found her at last. In a prison on the outskirts of Paris. My name is Rene Gallimard—also known as Madame Butterfly. *(He plunges the knife into his body)*

AUGUST SNOW

By Reynolds Price

August Snow *is the first play of Reynolds Price's* New Music *trilogy, which cumulatively spans two generations and forty years. In a speech addressed to the audience, twenty-two-year-old Porter Farwell remembers an epiphany he had eight years earlier, when a schoolteacher asked what he hoped to be.*

Note: Neal Avery is his best friend; they both work at Neal's family's store, Avery's Clothing.

PORTER: In a town this size, everybody's known your family since the Seven Years' War; so you have to live most of your life in code—little signals and fables for the kind and wise, not actual touch or plain true words. That's been all right by me most times; it keeps you from having to make up your mind too fast, or ever. For years you can walk around some strong magnet and never ask why or be told to explain. Then when you least expect it, somebody you've known from the dark of the womb will step up and reach for the trunk of your life and shake it like a cyclone, and you'll shed your apples in full public view.

It happened to me my first year in high school, fourteen years old—English class, of course. Miss Speed Brickhouse went round the room asking everybody what they hoped to be; and everybody answered some sensible way—storekeeper, bank teller, practical nurse. Then she called on me—"Porter, what's your plan?"

I was already helping at Avery's store—Neal and I on Saturdays—and I figured I'd sell men's clothing for life. But what I said was what slipped out. To Miss Speed's withered face, and twenty-six children vicious as bats, I said "I hope to be a lighthouse for others."

Miss Speed tried to save the day by saying the church was the noblest career, but everybody knew she was wrong, and they *howled*—right on through Commencement three whole years later.

I found the strength to hold my ground though, and I never explained. I knew I'd found, and told, the truth—a real light, for safety, in cold high seas. Not for *others* though; I lied in that—just for Neal Avery, the one I'd long since chosen as being in special need and worthy of care. I may well have failed.

THREE DAYS OF RAIN

By Richard Greenberg

Pip Wexler, an actor, is the son of a famous architect who died many years ago. His father's partner, the architect Edmund Janeway, has only recently passed away. Pip has been called for the reading of the will, along with Edmund Janeway's daughter and son, Nan and Walker. When Nan and Walker learn that Edmund has left Janeway House—a house he designed, and considered to be one of the great private residences of the last half-century—to Pip instead of them, Pip and Walker confront each other.

PIP: Why do you get to be the one who judges things when you're having the stupidest life of anybody? I'm sick of it, Walker. *You're* the one who's done the bad thing here, you're the one who ran off like a maniac and left us to go bonkers worrying about you. I've been good, Nan's been good, you've been bad. Okay, that's the morality of the situation. So you don't get to make the laws; that's the upshot. [. . .]

No, *I'm* talking now, and it's a very weird sensation. Look, Walker, look—it's just you can't be the only personality in the room anymore. You cannot just change the temperature of every circumstance by this kind of tyrannical psychosocial, you know, *fiat*—oh, *look*, I know you think I'm an idiot— [. . .] Yes, you did, you said it all the time, you just pretended sometimes not to mean it; but I know you meant it. [. . .] Even though *I* was the one who was off the charts in any standardized exam we ever took, while you were always getting lost on the way to the testing center. But that doesn't matter, I know— with your exquisite perversity that just *proves* it, but look, the fact is, it isn't true—being in a good mood is not the same thing as being a moron. It just isn't. And, you know, for years I wondered. I strove to sustain some level of unhappiness because I felt so left out but I couldn't manage it. [. . .] I don't know—I feel bad—I go to the gym—I feel better. Maybe that means I lack *gravitas* or something, but the hell with it, I'm having a good time. [. . .] Except I am no longer willing to bear the brunt of your *mean*ness. [. . .]

You know, it's not as if I don't know where it's coming from, it's not as if I don't know you've always been basically in love with me—that's been so obvious for so many years that— [. . .] I don't know what—but why does it have to be such a problem? Why couldn't we have just worked through it when we were eighteen? It would have been so easy. I would have been sensitive, you would have suffered for a while, it would have been over, and we could have spent the next fifteen years going to the movies or something like *people*. Instead of it fucking up everything. [. . .] Because it's just fucked up everything for such a long time—everything we had to keep from you— [. . .] . . . the stupid, gothic secrets—the tiptoeing around. [. . .] I mean, like all that time when Nan and I were sleeping together and in love and everything and we couldn't tell you because we were so afraid of how jealous you'd be, and we couldn't tell each other why we couldn't tell you because nobody was acknowledging any aspect of the situation—it was crazy, that felt awful—I hated lying to you. Like it or not, you're my oldest friend. I love you, you know, and what was the point? Everything is tolerable if you just *talk* about it, you know?

You know? *(Beat)* Was that *all* new information?

3

"TRYING TO TALK,
SAYING GOOD-BYE."

A QUESTION OF MERCY

By David Rabe

Inspired by Dr. Richard Selzer's New York Times Magazine essay about his personal experience with the issue of assisted suicide, David Rabe's play explores what happens when Anthony, stricken with AIDS, decides to end his life, and the effect of that decision on his survivors—including his lover Thomas and their dearest friend Susanah. Addressing the audience, Thomas describes what happened on the day the suicide was planned, when the three spent time together before leaving Anthony alone.

THOMAS: We actually went to a movie. In Princeton. The train makes a series of local stops. People get on and off at Newark and Metro Park and Metuchen. All different sizes and shapes of people. With everything hidden behind their eyes. The dinner the three of us shared was a weird, totally surreal experience. Susanah and me, trying to eat, while Anthony sipped water and stole glances at the clock. The three of us sitting there, trying to talk, saying good-bye. I thought about telling him that I could not permit things to go forward—I wanted to tell him that things had changed, that—but it seemed that if it was going to stop, he was the one to stop it. I kept sending him these messages with my eyes, to tell me what to do, looking at him for a sign that he was reconsidering, sifting his behavior for the slightest nuance of an invitation. It was like the first time that I kissed him. Who goes first?

Should I? Shouldn't I? Then I was in a cab. The cab was on the street. Susanah was reading *Time* magazine, and somewhere in that interlude, I started to imagine it all complete, all worked out. I imagined us returning to find him dead. It was hazy, a kind of cottony aftermath, the funeral, the tears. I imagined the crematorium and the fire—his ashes in a vase. I filled with love of him and an unearthly sadness, and then I imagined myself eating the ashes. I imagined the spoon and I imagined the taste of the ashes in my mouth. Susanah, I realized, was staring into my eyes, and we were in fact on the train. I don't know what she saw. Our friends in Princeton wanted us to go to a movie and have a late dinner. They met us at the station and we went straight to the movie.

GROSS INDECENCY:
THE THREE TRIALS OF OSCAR WILDE

By Moisés Kaufman

Moisés Kaufman's Gross Indecency: The Three Trials of Oscar Wilde *investigates the life, art and ultimate downfall of Oscar Wilde in the last five years of his life, focusing on the three trials that captivated England during the spring of 1895. The play takes place almost entirely in London's Old Bailey Central Criminal Court, with all the actors but one (Wilde) taking on multiple rolls and sharing the narration. Wilde himself initiated the first case, pursuing a prosecution for libel against his lover Lord Alfred Douglas's father, only to then be brought to court himself on the charge of "committing acts of gross indecency." He was tried twice, then convicted and sent to prison.*

Kaufman employs a journalistic, quasi-documentary style: the play quotes from the historical accounts that he used in his research, with the characters identifying the source material for the audience. Here, in a speech from Oscar Wilde: A Summing Up *by Lord Alfred Douglas, Douglas describes the aftermath of the first trial. During his description of the events, an auctioneer (played by one of the narrators) begins a public sale of items collected from Wilde's house. As the speech proceeds, Wilde enters the scene and Douglas shifts from talking about him to addressing Oscar directly.*

LORD ALFRED DOUGLAS: After Oscar's arrest, immediate ruin followed. He had two plays, *An Ideal Husband* and *The Importance of Being Earnest* running on the West End. He had been up till a week before the trial a comparatively rich man. Yet the moment he was arrested he was reduced to penury and assailed by all his creditors in a body while all his income simply stopped. He was of course condemned to pay all my father's costs; the managers suspended the performance of his plays; an execution was put in his house and furniture and effects were sold for a song. [. . .] The auction will begin with five lots: a collection of manuscripts of Oscar Wilde's poems. The original manuscripts of *The Portrait of Mr. W.H.* An autographed copy of *Dorian Gray.* Oscar Wilde's life-length portrait. A crayon drawing of a nude female by Whistler. On that day, Wilde's House Beautiful presented a pitiful picture: it was overrun by a whole crowd of curiosos, idlers and rumormongers. Doors were broken open, valuables were stolen, and the sale was carried on amidst scenes of chaotic disorder. Several original manuscripts mysteriously disappeared and have never since been discovered. [. . .] From affluence he passed suddenly to dire poverty at a time when money was needed for his defense. [. . .] Oscar was imprisoned in Holloway Gaol as he waited for his trial.

I used to see him there every day in the ghastly way that visits are arranged in prisons. The visitor goes into a box rather like the box in a pawn shop. There is a whole row of these boxes, each occupied by a visitor and opposite, the prisoner. [. . .] We were separated by a corridor about a yard in width and a warder passes up and down between us. *(Shouting)* We had to shout to make our voices heard above the voices of other prisoners and visitors. Nothing more revolting and cruel and deliberately malignant could be devised by human ingenuity. Poor Oscar was rather deaf. He could hardly hear what I said in this Tower of Babel. He looked at me with tears running down his cheeks and I looked at him. [. . .] Oscar, I know I always advised you to fight my father, but I am not impervious to reason. If Clarke had assured me that you had no chance, and were merely cutting your own throat and playing into my father's hands, I would have been convinced, Oscar. I never intended for this to happen. [. . .]

Oscar and his legal advisors urged me to go to France before the second trial. They assured me that my presence in the country could only do Oscar harm. They said that if I were to be called to the witness stand, I should infallibly destroy what small chance he had for acquittal. His solicitors also told me that unless I left the country, Sir Edward Clarke, who was now defending Wilde for no charge, would throw up his defense. So I embarked for France on the day before the trial, the 25th of April 1895. It would be two years before I was to see him again.

GROSS INDECENCY: THE THREE TRIALS OF OSCAR WILDE

By Moisés Kaufman

The following speech, from the start of the third trial, is taken from Wilde's De Profundis, *the long emotional letter he wrote to Lord Alfred Douglas, his friend and lover, from his prison cell. As Wilde speaks, a series of witnesses step forward throughout the speech to testify that he committed acts of "gross indecency with male persons." Wilde is "exhausted, desperate." Kaufman's stage directions indicate the sound of a beating heart rising in a gradual crescendo throughout this speech.*

OSCAR WILDE: I remember when I was sitting in the dock on my last trial, listening to Lockwood's appalling denunciation of me—like a thing out of Tacitus, like a passage in Dante— and being sickened with horror at what I heard. [. . .]

I must say to myself that I ruined myself, and that nobody great or small can be ruined except by their own hand. This pitiless indictment I bring without pity against myself. I let myself be lured into long spells of senseless and sensual ease. [. . .] I surrounded myself with the smaller natures and the meaner minds. I became the spendthrift of my genius. I grew careless of the lives of others. I took pleasure where it pleased me and passed on. [. . .] I forgot that every little action of the common day makes or unmakes character, and that therefore what one does in the secret chamber one has some day to cry aloud on the housetops. [. . .] I blame myself terribly. As I sit a ruined man, it is myself I blame. [. . .] While there is nothing wrong in what I did, there is something wrong in what I became. [. . .] How weary I am of the whole thing, of the shame and the struggling and the hatred. To see those people coming into the box one after the other to witness against me makes me sick. [. . .]

Reason does not help me. It tells me that the law under which I'm being judged is a wrong and unfair law, and the system under which I'm suffering, a wrong and unjust system. [. . .] The world is growing more tolerant. One day you will be ashamed of your treatment of me. [. . .] I feel inclined to stretch out my hands and cry to them: do what you will with me, in God's name, only do it quickly. Can you not see I'm worn out? If hatred gives you pleasure, indulge it.

UNFINISHED STORIES

By Sybille Pearson

Walter, an eighty-year-old German immigrant, lives with Gaby, the former wife of his son, Yves. Walter is physically frail, but also tough and determined; he hides his pain from his family—including Yves, with whom he shares a relationship that is tenuous at best, and his adored grandson Daniel. Walter, a former doctor, has planned his own death. In this speech, he asks Daniel to bear witness to his living will.

Note: "nanu" is an indefinable German sigh or explanation; "opa" is German for grandfather.

WALTER: You see, my boy, in hospitals, on the many benches, sit the estranged . . . fathers, sons, mothers, husbands . . . incapable of allowing each other to die. "Let him see me once more. Let him open his eyes once more." This they say to their doctor, to me. In that "once more," love will be shown, finally exchanged. I am to put a tube in him. One here. One here. Keep him for me. You understand. Nanu. Which agony? You are the doctor. Which agony do you treat? Your patient's? Who needs to die, to be released from this pain. Or the agony of the man or the woman who's waited for love too long? The patient didn't leave a statement with his wishes. [. . .]

Nanu. Now we are a different story. I have no wish to live. I will not see the end of this disease. I know how it ends. I have seen it too often. I tell you this. I have a statement here that needs a witness. You say you will be it. You sign. I ask you not to ask me more questions. I ask you to play chess. You do. We play a game of chess. We say good night. I go to my room. I've had brandy. I inject morphine. Perhaps in the morning, I still breathe. Gaby finds me. She cannot let me die as I wish. She cannot be without hope. Nanu. In the hospital, you show the doctor my note. "Yes," he'll say, "but what happened that day?" You will tell him a family argument in the afternoon. That I asked if Yves called. That he didn't. He is a romantic this doctor. Decides that was the reason I took morphine. There are people like this. He will tell you of a machine that will give me what he calls the gift of time, enough time, he tells you, so I might see this new child. And will you think, There will be a new grandchild, a good one, the better one. I will be the one to take him from Opa? That test will be harder than what we do here. *(He holds paper out to Daniel)* I am dependent on you. Dependent on my evaluation of you.

4

"ONCE YOU KNOW YOU'RE DEAD, WHY KEEP ON DYIN . . ."

THE COLORED MUSEUM

By George C. Wolfe

The Colored Museum *is set in a "museum where the myths and madness of black/Negro/colored Americans are stored." In this exuberant satire, the characters—who are the "exhibits"—must navigate between recognizing the pain caused by a legacy of oppression without being defined by it in the present. In the "Soldier with a Secret" exhibit, we meet Junie Robinson, a combat solider who is "somewhat dimwitted" but with "an easygoing charm about him." Printed in its entirety, this speech is Junie's only appearance in the play.*

JUNIE: Pst. Pst. I know the secret. The secret to your pain. Course I didn't always know. First I had to die, then come back to life, 'fore I had the gift. Ya see the Cappin sent me off up ahead to scout for screamin yella bastards. Course for the life of me I couldn't understand why they'd be screamin seein as how we was tryin to kill them and they us. But anyway, I'm off looking, when all of a sudden I find myself caught smack dead in the middle of this explosion. This blindin, burnin, scaldin, explosion. Musta been a booby trap or something, 'cause all around me is fire. Hell I'm on fire. Like a piece of chicken dropped in a skillet of cracklin grease. Why my flesh was justa peelin off of my bones. But then I says to myself, "Junie, if yo flesh is on fire, how come you don't feel no pain. And I didn't. I swear as I'm standin here, I felt nuthin. That's when I sort of put two and two together and realized I didn't feel no whole lot of hurtin 'cause I done died.

Well I just picked myself up an walked right on out of that explosion. Hell once you know you're dead, why keep on dyin, ya know. So like I say, I walk right outta that explosion, fully expectin to see white clouds, Jesus and my mama, only all I saw was more war. Shootin goin on way off in this direction and that direction. And there, standin around, was all the guys. Hubert, J.F., the Cappin. I guess the sound of the explosion must of attracted 'em and they all starin at me like I'm some kind of ghost. So I yells to 'em, "Hey there Hubert! Hey there Cappin!" But they just stare. So I tells 'em how I'd died and how I guess it wasn't my time 'cause here I am, "Fully in the flesh and not a scratch to my bones." And they still just stare. So I took to starin back. *(The expression on his face slowly turns to horror and disbelief)* Only what I saw . . . well, I can't exactly to this day describe it. But I swear, as sure as they was wearin green and holdin guns, they was each wearin a piece of the future on their faces. Yeah. All the hurt that was gonna get done to them and they was gonna do to folks was right there clear as day. I saw how J.F., once he got back to Chicago, was gonna get shot by this po-lice, and I saw how Hubert was gonna start beatin up on his old lady which I didn't understand, 'cause all he could do was talk on and on about how much he loved her. Each and every one of 'em had pain in his future and blood on his path. And God or the devil one spoke to me and said, "Junie, these colored boys ain't gonna be the same after this war. They ain't gonna have no kind of happiness."

Well, right then and there it come to me. The secret to their pain. Late that night, after the medics done checked me over and found me fit for fightin, after everybody done settle down for the night, I sneaked over to where Hubert was sleepin, and with a needle I stole from the medics . . . pst pst . . . I shot a little air into his veins. The second he died, all the hurtin-to-come just left his face. *(He smiles)* Two weeks later I got J.F. and after that Woodrow . . . Jimmy Joe . . . I even spent all night waitin by the latrine 'cause I knew the Cappin always made a late-night visit and pst . . . pst . . . I got him. *(Quite proud of himself)* That's how come I died and come back to life. 'Cause just like Jesus went around healin the sick, I'm supposed to go around healin the hurtin all these colored boys wearin from the war. Pst. Pst. I know the secret. The secret to your pain. The secret to yours, and yours. Pst. Pst. Pst. Pst.

THE SPEED OF DARKNESS

By Steve Tesich

Lou, a homeless Vietnam veteran, spends most of his time following a touring Vietnam memorial as it moves around the country. It brings him to South Dakota, where he shows up on the doorstep of his old friend Joe, a fellow veteran he has not seen for eighteen years. During the war, Joe saved Lou's life; that story, and its consequences, are described by Joe in the monologues on the following pages. Before Lou moves on, he tells Joe about the day they "unveiled or whatever they call it" the Vietnam War Memorial in Washington, D.C.

Note: Mary is Joe's teenage daughter.

LOU: You can relax, Joe. That's what I plan to do. I'll be leaving in a few minutes. [. . .] It's like this. When you show up, you can show up any old way, but when you leave, you have to leave right. After what your Mary did for me, I don't think I could say good-bye to her without lying and saying, "I'll see you soon," or something like that. I don't want to lie to her. [. . .] You never did come to Washington, did you? When they unveiled or whatever they call it, the real one. [. . .] I looked for you that day. [. . .] All the vets were there. [. . .] Like big stone pages from some book, that's what it looked like. Page after page. I was hoping to find my name on one of them. [. . .] I made the papers the next day. I got so upset when I couldn't find my name there, I tried to scratch it in stone with my can opener. These two marine guards dragged me away. They didn't hurt me or nothing. Very nice boys and kind of sorry they had to be doing what they were doing. I'm an MIA boys, missing in America. Give me an address. "We can't let you do that, sir." Sir, they called me. Wonderful boys. Perfect marines. "We can't let you do that, sir. The Wall's only for those who died. Not for those who survived, sir." Boys, I told them, I swear to you on my word of honor, I didn't survive. If you don't believe me, just ask some of these vets here who knew me when I was alive. They'll tell you. Anyway, I made the papers. No picture. Just a little story. Disturbed vet tries to desecrate the memorial. It hurt when I read that. *(He stands up suddenly)* I guess I better get going. [. . .] I might change my mind if I wait. You saved my life. I can't betray you. And I can't do anything without betraying you.

THE SPEED OF DARKNESS

By Steve Tesich

Happily married with a beautiful teenage daughter, Joe is a successful businessman who was recently named South Dakota's Man of the Year. He is a veteran who seems to have escaped the shadow of Vietnam. But when his old war buddy Lou shows up unexpectedly on his doorstep after eighteen years, Joe's carefully held together life suddenly starts to unravel. At the end of the play, he finally breaks down and reveals to his wife—and especially his daughter—the truth of what happened to him and Lou and another soldier, Benny, during the war. During this speech, Tesich writes in a stage direction, "The sun will set while he speaks. It will become twilight and then it will become night. We should feel this change."

JOE: There was nothing special about us. We were like all the other guys. We did what they did. They'd tell us to go someplace. And we went. They'd tell us to go somewhere else and we went there. And then a night came. Like any other night. And we were out there in the night where they'd sent us. There were trees when we got there, but then it got so dark we couldn't see no trees anymore. And then we hear 'em coming. *(A beat as he listens)* Far away, but we hear 'em. Airplanes. We know they're ours, 'cause the other side don't have no airplanes. And they're coming closer. Flying low. We're all looking up. Watching. Closer and closer. Hurts the ears, they're so loud. Like being in a box with a lid of noise on top of your head. And then the whole box shakes and shudders and there's suddenly fire everywhere. The trees we couldn't see. We see 'em now. They're burning like kerosene rags. Those planes. Our own planes are dropping stuff on us. We run. We run from the fire, but there's something worse than fire. There's this smell. And there's something horrible about that smell. So we're running, but we're trying not to breathe because there's something in the air that scares us. Lou's there. Benny's there. I see their faces. I see 'em real clear 'cause those trees are burning. And they look mad. It's like they've got rabies or something. And I know my face looks like theirs. And we're running. Trying not to breathe. And it feels like we're running in a box. Lou gets hurt and falls down. Benny, he can't run anymore. So I put Lou on my back and I drag Benny by the arm. Over bodies, through muck and fire, holding my breath and then I just can't do it anymore. Can't run no more. All three of us. We're still thinking running, but we're not moving. We're just twitching. Our faces are still running. The flesh on them is grimacing and trying to rip itself off the bones and run away from us, but we can't budge. All we can do is twitch and try not to breathe that air, but we're breathing it. We know it's doing us in, but we're breathing it in. Oh, God! I start screaming. Dear God, please. Save us! And Lou and Benny, they think I got the answer and they join me. The three of us. There. On our knees. Pleading with God. Save us. Please. Save us from our own. *(A beat of silence)* We weren't saved. But we were rescued. That's what they called what they did to us the next morning. They called it rescued. They flew us to a hospital. They gave us these chemicals and things. They used these big X-ray-type machines on us to try and kill the poison the planes had dropped inside of us and in the process we were sterilized. A little side effect of the cure. Nobody told us. They told us we were fine. Good as new. So there we were. Me, Lou and Benny. Walking down this long corridor in the hospital. Far down the corridor, there's this glass door. On the other side of the door: sunshine. We're walking real fast. Sunshine. We're almost racing each other. All we got to do is get out there in the sun and everything will be all right again. We run through the door and the door shuts behind us. And I stand there in the warm sunlight. It's so warm and bright and I'm trying to smile and be happy. But suddenly I know. I feel it. I'm out, but something didn't come out with me. It got left behind. It was gone.

THE SPEED OF DARKNESS

By Steve Tesich

This monologue is from the end of Steve Tesich's drama about the aftermath of the Vietnam War and its effect on the veterans who returned home. Joe has finally broken down, revealing (in his previous speech) that his own government sterilized him and—in this confession to his wife Anne and their daughter—the revenge that he and his friend Lou took as a result.

JOE: I was dying for a family, but I knew where things stood with me. I love you, but I wanted you to move on. But then you said: Joe, I'm gonna have a baby. I could tell you wanted to tell me more, but I didn't wanna hear more. A miracle!

I told myself. That's what it is. A miracle. One last little living seed inside me managed to survive somehow. Lou! I hugged him. Lou, I'm gonna marry Annie. I'm gonna be a father. And Lou, he was my buddy and he wanted to believe in miracles and he let me believe. But it's hard to cling to a miracle when you're sober. So in order to cling, we started drinking. There were no regular jobs for us after the war. Me and Lou, we just didn't look regular enough. But there were jobs. There were these fine, upstanding companies looking for a few good men who didn't ask no questions. They had stuff they wanted dumped and they didn't care where. Big black oil drums full of it. We knew we were handling scary stuff. But we weren't scared. We weren't scared of nothing anymore. We got paid by the barrel and paid real good and stayed real drunk. On nights like this, we drove up there. There are cracks and holes and crevices on top of the mesa and into them we dumped the stuff from the oil drums. It was like dumping death by the barrel, we knew there was death inside of 'em, but it felt good to do it. We were getting even. It was war again, only this time we were dumping stuff on our own. And just like it felt good to love you by day, Annie, just like that, it felt good to get drunk and hate by night and dump that death into the holes. Down the hatch! I couldn't wait for the sun to set, so I could get drunk and hate again. Me and Lou, we'd crack jokes while we did it and we tried to goad each other on. Mother Earth, Lou called the mesa. I called it Mother Country. Here you go, Mom. Have another one on us. Night after night, week after week, for over five months, we did that, but no matter how much we tried to hate, it still wasn't enough. We wanted to hate more. There was more venom in us than in all those oil drums put together. The kind of hate that desecrates life. Some eternal hate is what we wanted. To get even for everything. And on our last night up there, we found a way to hate. We stood on top of these empty oil drums. We were grinning at each other, as we dropped our pants down around our knees. And we grabbed ourselves and we cursed while we did what we did. Here you go, Mom. Here you go. And we shot out dead seed into those dark holes full of death already. Here you go, Mom. Let's see the children that are born from this. Here's your next generation, Mom. Let's see how you like them sons and daughters. I wished all that. I wished that horror with all my heart. But I don't want it no more. I wanna take it back. I wanna take it back and I don't know how. I can't bear it. My heart is . . . *(He cries out in pain)*

5

"SOME SENSE OF HISTORY."

PTERODACTYLS

By Nicky Silver

In this black comedy, playwright Nicky Silver says, "Broad comedy and utter despair are juxtaposed . . . but not blended." After an absence of five years—and having recently been diagnosed with AIDS—Todd Duncan has returned home to his wealthy, supremely dysfunctional family. Todd, twenty-three, is asymptomatic and outwardly healthy. He stands before an easel on which is propped a map of the earth, addressing the audience. This is the beginning of the play.

TODD: In the beginning, there were dinosaurs. Lots of dinosaurs. And they were big. They were very, very large—in comparison to man they were. They were huge. And there were many different kinds. There were ceratops and stegosauruses. There was the tyrannosaurus and the pterodactyl. And they lived, not in harmony, roaming the earth at will, raping, as it were, the planet and pillaging without regard. And, and um . . . uh . . . *(He loses his place and quickly checks his pockets for notes)* Um, I seem to have forgotten my notes. I'm sorry. I thought I left them in my pocket. Maybe I wasn't supposed to wear this. Maybe I left them on the table. Maybe I—oh well, it doesn't matter now. I don't have them. That's the point. I think I remember most of it—maybe I left them—it doesn't matter. Where was I? Oh, yes. It got cold. That's right, it got very, very cold and all the dinosaurs died. They all died. At once. It got cold and they died. And the land masses shifted and arranged themselves into the pattern we see now on the map. Basically. I think. There weren't any divisions for countries or states or anything, and I'm sure California was bigger, but it resembled what's on the map. During the cold spell, which is generally referred to as "the ice age"—or maybe it was before the ice age, or after it—I can't remember—but life started spontaneously. In a lake. Here, I think. *(He indicates the Sea of Japan)* And amoebas multiplied and became fish—don't ask me how—which evolved into monkeys. And then one day, the monkeys stood up, erect, realized they had opposing thumbs and developed speech. Thus, Mankind was born. Here. *(He indicates Africa)* Some people liked Africa, so they stayed there and became black. Some people left, looking for something, and became Europeans. And the Europeans forgot about the Africans and made countries and Queen Elizabeth executed her own half-sister Mary Queen of Scots. Some Europeans were Jewish, but most were Christians of some kind, Jesus having been born some time prior—oops, I forgot that. I'm sorry. Jesus was born. And there were other religions, too, but I can't remember very much about them, so I'm sure they weren't very important. During the Renaissance people got very fat. Picasso sculpted *David*, Marco Polo invented pizza, Columbus discovered the New World and Gaetan Dugas discovered the Fountain of Youth. Europeans imported tea, to drink, and Africans, to do their work. Edison invented the telephone, Martha Graham invented modern dance. Hitler invented fascism and Rose Kennedy invented nepotism. Orson Welles made *Citizen Kane* and mothers loved their children, who rebelled, when the sun shined most of the time, except when it rained and there was a rhythm to our breathing. There was an order to the world. And I was born here. *(He indicates Philadelphia)* I give you this brief summary of events, this overview, so you'll have some perspective. I'm sure I got some of it wrong. I've lost my notes, but it's basically the idea. And I wanted you to have, I think, some sense of history.

THE AMERICA PLAY

By Suzan-Lori Parks

Six years after The America Play *was published, Suzan-Lori Parks was asked about Abraham Lincoln in an* American Theatre *magazine interview. "You're not done with Lincoln, are you?" was the question, to which Parks replied, "No, I'm not—or I should say, he's not done with me." The central character in* The America Play *is an African-American man who makes his living as a Lincoln impersonator; he dresses as the president, and is shot over and over again by paying customers who pretend to be John Wilkes Booth. This first monologue is from the beginning of the play, when The Foundling Father (or Lesser Known) introduces himself to the audience.*

Note: the "(Rest)," an aspect of what Parks understatedly calls her use of "slightly unconventional theatrical elements," signifies "a little time, a pause, a breather," a transition for the actor and the character.

THE FOUNDLING FATHER AS ABRAHAM LINCOLN: There was once a man who was told that he bore a strong resemblance to Abraham Lincoln. He was tall and thinly built just like the Great Man. His legs were the longer part just like the Great Mans legs. His hands and feet were large as the Great Mans were large. The Lesser Known had several beards which he carried around in a box. The beards were his although he himself had not grown them on his face but since he'd secretly bought the hairs from his barber and arranged their beard shapes and since the procurement and upkeep of his beards took so much work he figured that the beards were completely his. Were as authentic as he was, so to speak. His beard box was of cherry wood and lined with purple velvet. He had the initials "A.L." tooled in gold on the lid. *(Rest)*

While the Great Mans livelihood kept him in Big Town the Lesser Knowns work kept him in Small Town. The Great Man by trade was a president. The Lesser Known was a Digger by trade. From a family of Diggers. Digged graves. He was known in Small Town to dig his graves quickly and neatly. This brought him a steady business.

(Rest)

A wink to Mr. Lincolns pasteboard cutout. *(He winks at Lincolns pasteboard cutout)*

(Rest)

It would be helpful to our story if when the Great Man died in death he were to meet the Lesser Known. It would be helpful to our story if, say, the Lesser Known were summoned to Big Town by the Great Mans wife: *"Emergency* oh, *Emergency,* please put the Great Man in the ground" (they say the Great Mans wife was given to hysterics: one young son dead others sickly: even the Great Man couldnt save them: a war on then off and surrendered to: "Play Dixie I always liked that song": the brother against the brother: a new nation all conceived and ready to be hatched: the Great Man takes to guffawing guffawing at thin jokes in bad plays: "You sockdologizing old man-trap!" haw haw haw because he wants so very badly to laugh at something and one moment guffawing and the next moment the Great Man is gunned down. In his rocker. "Useless Useless" and there were bills to pay.) *"Emergency,* oh *Emergency* please put the Great Man in the ground."

(Rest)

It is said that the Great Mans wife did call out and it is said that the Lesser Known would sneak away from his digging and stand behind a tree where he couldnt be seen or get up and leave his wife and child after the blessing had been said and the meat carved during the distribution of the vegetables it is said that he would leave his wife and standing in the kitchen or sometimes out in the yard between the right angles of the house stand out there where he couldnt be seen stand-

ing with his ear cocked. *"Emergency,* oh, *Emergency,* please put the Great Man in the ground."
(Rest)
It would help if she had called out and if he had been summoned been given a ticket all bought and paid for and boarded a train in his look-alike black frock coat bought on time and already exhausted. Ridiculous. If he had been summoned. Been summoned between the meat and the vegetables and boarded a train to Big Town where he would line up and gawk at the Great Mans corpse along with the rest of them. But none of this was meant to be.
(Rest)
A nod to the bust of Mr. Lincoln. *(He nods to the bust of Lincoln)*
But none of this was meant to be. For the Great Man had been murdered long before the Lesser Known had been born. Howuhboutthat. So that any calling that had been done he couldnt hear, any summoning he had hoped for he couldnt answer but somehow not even unheard and unanswered because he hadnt even been there although you should note that he talked about the murder and the mourning that followed as if he'd been called away on business at the time and because of the business had missed it. Living regretting he hadnt arrived sooner. Being told from birth practically that he and the Great Man were dead ringers, more or less, and knowing that he, if he had been in the slightest vicinity back then, would have had at least a chance at the great honor of digging the Great Mans grave.

THE AMERICA PLAY

By Suzan-Lori Parks

This monologue, a latter part of the previous speech, describes how The Foundling Father became famous. A Lincoln impersonator, he makes his living in "a great hole," a replica of a theme park called The Great Hole of History. (See previous speech for a note about the "(Rest).")

THE FOUNDLING FATHER AS ABRAHAM LINCOLN: The Lesser Known left his wife and child and went out West finally. Between the meat and the vegetables. A momentous journey. Enduring all the elements. Without a friend in the world. And the beasts of the forest took him in. He got there and he got his plot he staked his claim he tried his hand at his own Big Hole. As it had been back East everywhere out West he went people remarked on his likeness to Lincoln. How, in a limited sort of way, taking into account of course his natural God-given limitations, how he was identical to the Great Man in gait and manner how his legs were long and torso short. The Lesser Known had by this time taken to wearing a false wart on his cheek in remembrance of the Great Mans wart. When the Westerners noted his wart they pronounced the 2 men in virtual twinship.
(Rest)
Goatee. Huh. Goatee
(Rest)
"He digged the Hole and the Whole held him."
(Rest)
"I cannot dig, to beg I am ashamed."
(Rest)
The Lesser Known had under his belt a few of the Great Mans words and after a day of digging, in the evenings, would stand in his hole reciting. But the Lesser Known was a curiosity at

best. None of those who spoke of his virtual twinship with greatness would actually pay money to watch him be that greatness. One day he tacked up posters inviting them to come and throw old food at him while he spoke. This was a moderate success. People began to save their old food "for Mr. Lincoln" they said. He took to traveling playing small towns. Made money. And when someone remarked that he played Lincoln so well that he ought to be shot, it was as if the Great Mans footsteps had been suddenly revealed:

(Rest)

The Lesser Known returned to his hole and, instead of speeching, his act would now consist of a single chair, a rocker, in a dark box. The public was invited to pay a penny, choose from the selection of provided pistols, enter the darkened box and "shoot Mr. Lincoln." The Lesser Known became famous overnight.

INSURRECTION: HOLDING HISTORY

By Robert O'Hara

Asked in an American Theatre *interview what his impetus was for writing this play, Robert O'Hara answered, "I woke up crying one night from a dream about my grandfather, who is dead, asking me to take him home, and I knew when he said 'home,' he meant* home, *back to slavery, to that place where it all began for us in this country. I gave his name, T.J., to the grandfather in* Insurrection." *A 189-year-old former slave, T.J. has inhabited a wheelchair for the past century. When he takes his great-great-grandson Ron back in time to Nat Turner's rebellion, Ron tries to stop the massacre that he knows will take place. T.J., who lived through Turner's uprising, tells Ron he must learn from the past but move forward into his own future.*

T.J.:
　　slavery.
　　ends.
　　ronnie.
　　[. . .]
　　HUSH UP!
　　you know nuthin
　　you know letters on paper
　　you know big words
　　connected ta little ideas
　　you know nuthin
　　i killed a man this afternoon
　　wit'out a thought
　　wit'out hesitation
　　i killed that son of a bitch because it was either him o'
　　　　you
　　and. YOU. mine.
　　i didn't need no mo' time i didn't need no mo' thinkin' I
　　　　didn't have no plan
　　DEATH ain't nuthin new ta me n' it ain't new ta them
　　　　slaves
　　i LIVED it!!
　　you. the one Watchin'!
　　i brought you heah ta learn. ta listen. not change nuthin
　　we change in oura OWN time.
　　not. in. othas.
　　you wake up ev'ry mornin' breathin' the AIR that NAT
　　TURNER fought fo' you ta breathe and you sleep ev'ry
　　nite wit no FEAR cuz that crazy. nigga. SHOUTED Out
　　at the Moon askin' his Gawd fo' a way thru dis trouble
　　and you think you can show up back heah and BLOCK
　　that!!! ronnie you are who you are because them people
　　that's gon' git shot up hung up cut up is what will 'llow
　　you ta enter them doors of that fancy college ya go ta
　　read them wordy books and write them thesis papers

SEE these niggas heah cain't understand that ALL they
know is that they wanna be FREE and that's what they
plannin' ta Do
So they gon' WIN
they might DIE
but they gon' WIN
You. da Proof.
slavery.
ends.

MISS EVERS' BOYS

By David Feldshuh

Miss Evers' Boys *is based on a true event in American histo-*
ry—the now infamous Tuskegee Study conducted in Alabama
in the 1930s, in which nearly four hundred African-American
men were secretly denied treatment for syphilis and deliber-
ately lied to by public health officials. Eugene Brodus, an
African-American doctor, is the administrative head of the
hospital in which the study was conducted. He is a good man
who believes the study will scientifically prove that there is no
biological racial difference, merely racial bias. In this speech,
he tries to convince Miss Evers, a nurse, to continue partici-
pating in the study despite her desire to tell the men "the
straight truth."

BRODUS: I once did two autopsies at the same time. On two
patients, both in their thirties. On two tables. Laid out next to
each other. I took out the hearts and put them on a scale and
weighed them both. Together. Then I went about some other
business. When I came back I realized I hadn't tagged those
hearts. I didn't know which one came from which table. Now

that was more than embarrassing. You see there was a white man laid out on one table and a colored man on the other. Now if I put the white heart in the colored patient . . . Or the colored heart in the white patient . . . So I looked at those two hearts for a long time. I held them both up in my hands, examining them. For the longest time . . . Then I closed my eyes and put a heart in each body and sewed them up. As simple as that. *(Pause)* Nurse Evers, you and I got a chance to do something special right now. We got a chance to push people to see things in a way they've never seen them before. Push them to see past the hate, past the idea of difference . . . Isn't that what we've got to do?

THREE SISTERS

By Anton Chekhov
Adapted by David Mamet

David Mamet's adaptation of The Three Sisters *remains true to Chekhov's play: Vershinin is still an idealistic army commander, in love with Masha but bound to his own unhappy marriage. The style—the pauses, the emphasis, the declarative language—is pure David Mamet. Here, Vershinin describes the fire that nearly destroyed his house, and the town. He speaks to Tuzenbach, a fellow soldier; Masha's sister Irina; Masha's husband Kulygin—and to Masha herself, who enters midway through his recounting of the fire's terror.*

VERSHININ: I ran home. When the fire broke out. I raced home. As I got there, I saw the house was safe. But my girls, my little girls—they were out on the threshold. Dressed in their thin underclothes. Their mother wasn't there. Everywhere people running. Horses, dogs running . . . I saw on their faces such terror. Such terror. It broke my heart. My *God* the things those little girls will have to face in the course of their lives. *(Pause)* What they will have to live through. And I came here. *(Pause)* And here is their mother.

My little girls. Were stranded at the threshold. And the street was red with fire. And there was. That terrible noise. And I thought: long ago . . . long ago . . . that *something like this* has occurred. *(Pause)* There was a raid. An enemy . . . "invaded" . . . they looted. And killed and plundered. *(Pause)* In a savage time. And I thought: in essence, what difference is there? Between that time and this? *(Pause)* Between what *was* and *is* . . . ? And then more time will pass. Two, and three hundred years. Will have passed. And *our* life. Our . . . "shouting" . . . will be looked back on with the same . . . "incredulity" as that which *we* have. Looking at the past. How odd it seems. How *awkward*. How strange. *(Pause)* Yes. Forgive me. It seems that I'm "going on again." I am philosophizing. *(Pause)*

Listen to me. It seems . . . what if . . . as if everyone in the town were sleeping. Can you feel that? As if that were so? As if only we three in the town were awake. Truly awake. But. In each generation. As time passed. More would come. Gradually. Constantly. Until the *people*, you see, gradually, would come 'round to think your way. Until this state of "wakefulness," over the years, until it came to be, you see . . . the "norm." Until that norm *itself* was surpassed. In "Time" . . . do you see . . . ? In "time" . . . and people. Who were born. Looked back . . . they looked back . . . *(Pause) Ha. (Pause) Lord*, I want to live . . . I'm in a mood, I know it . . . I would like to live to see it . . . *HA*. But I want to live . . .

6

"HERE I AM, TALKING TO YOU ABOUT MY REVOLUTIONARY LIFE."

THE DAY YOU'LL LOVE ME

By José Ignacio Cabrujas
Translated by Eduardo Machado

Pio Miranda is a schoolteacher in Caracas, Venezuela, in 1935. He dreams of marrying Maria Luisa and taking her away with him to Stalin's Ukraine, where they will live a revolutionary life in a true proletarian land. He tells her sister—who does not trust his intentions—the story of why he became a Communist.

PIO: In the thirty-nine years of my life, I have been a schoolteacher, a printing shop cashier, a secretary for an emerald buyer on the Rio Magdalena, a spiritualist, a Rosicrucian, a Freemason, an atheist, a libertarian and a Communist. I'm a Communist because when I was a boy, in Valencia, my sainted mother, Ernestina, the widow of Miranda, a retired nurse at the Lepers' Hospital, and a constant reader of *The Count of Monte Cristo,* hanged herself in her room. Do you know how she hanged herself? She piled up on her floor *Les Misérables* by Victor Hugo, *The Thirteenth Coach* by Xavier de Montepin, *The Lady of the Camelias* by Alexander Dumas, *Anna Karenina* by Leo Tolstoy and an illustrated edition of the Bible. She got up on the pile of books and, God damn it, didn't even leave me a word of explanation. She just leapt from romantic literature with an all-consuming fury. Now it seems a joke, and I surprise myself sometimes laughing when I tell it. But from that day on I was afraid! I would wet the bed from sheer anxiety. I didn't dare cross the patio after eleven for fear of meeting up with her under the lemon tree, or in the dining room, or in the kitchen. You ask, what the hell am I afraid of? I'm afraid she'd tell me why she did it. I'm afraid of ending up on the same beam under the same roof. *(Small pause)* I read the books from that scaffold Mama had made in her room, looking for some key, some answer, any explanation whatsoever! And I found nothing. Pages and pages . . . of fluff. *(Pause)* I joined the seminary of the archdiocese and began to masturbate every night. One day they discovered me in the middle of a lark with a statue of Santa Rita. And they had me declared afflicted and insane! So I stopped believing in God. Because how the fuck can I believe in God if a statue of Santa Rita turns me on? Don't you understand that they expelled me from this provincial life? [. . .] There is no merciful Lord! You are in the world with your hands and your tongue . . . And there is no merciful Lord! I could try to tell you that I'm a Communist because of the ballsiness of the *Manifesto*, or the courage of Marx, or the thinking of Engels! But I am a Communist because of the statement of Aura Celina Sarabia who was the cook in the Hotel Bolivar where my mother died. And do you know why my mother hanged herself? Because they reduced the budget of the Ministry of Health, and there was a mistake in the list of the people with pensions! Aura Celina told me. A mistake in the list of pensioners, and six weeks without any money. She died of shame . . . And I asked myself, how can I destroy these institutions and somebody told me, "Read this." And here I am, talking to you about my revolutionary life.

PRINCIPIA SCRIPTORIAE

By Richard Nelson

Ernesto Pico, in his early twenties, is one of two young writers being held in a Latin American prison. Early in the play he tells Bill, an American, about what it was like studying in England at Cambridge University. To begin, he tells the story of his mother and the brothels.

ERNESTO: It's not at all like everyone says it is. [. . .] They're not all homosexual. [. . .] You wouldn't believe the bizarre conversations my mother and I had before I left. It is not often that a son gets such a clear picture of just how his mother's mind works. There is a good reason for that. There is a humane reason for that. *(Short pause)* Here is this nice upper-middle-class lady—and what does she start to do: take her only son around to brothels. [. . .] Mind you, the better brothels, but still. [. . .] I'm not saying she went in. God forbid. She just took me around. [. . .] No. She stayed outside. She just hung around outside. And paid. *(Laughs)* This is true. There can be some really strange shit down here. People can be really fucked up down here. [. . .] She'd pay and stay outside. But first they'd have to haggle though. I'm standing there and they are haggling over the price. My mother and the prostitute. *(Short pause)* That sort of does something to one's sense of pride. *(Short pause)* And none of it would have happened if the priest hadn't told her about English universities. The ideas people get into their heads. [. . .] Especially when you're talking about a place they've never been. Like Cambridge. Or Oxford. [. . .] That's not to say that some shit doesn't happen at English universities. Of course it does, but hell no one is pushing anyone around, they've still got English manners after all. Now there's something you don't find here. [. . .] Still, it turned that there were prostitutes even in Cambridge. So I wrote my mother that and she raised my allowance.

THE BALTIMORE WALTZ

By Paula Vogel

Diagnosed with Acquired Toilet Disease, a fatal affliction that seems to strike only single schoolteachers, Anna sets off on a whirlwind tour of Europe so that "in whatever time is left she can fuck her brains out." In Holland, she goes to bed with The Little Dutch Boy at Age 50. "He wears traditional wooden shoes, trousers and vest. His Buster Brown haircut and hat make him look dissipated."

THE LITTLE DUTCH BOY AT AGE 50: It was kermistime, the festival in my village. And I had too much bier with my school friends, Piet and Jan. Ja. Soo—Piet thought we should go to the outer dyke with cans of spray paint, after the kermis. So we went.

Here in Noord Holland there are three walls of defenses against the cruelty of the North Sea. The first dyke is called the Waker—the Watcher; the second dyke is de Slaper—the Sleeper; and the last dyke, which had never before been tested, is known as the Dromer—the Dreamer. At the kermis the older folk were much worried—the sea had been rising, and the dunes and helm were already overtaken by the flood.

And when we got the Dreamer, Piet said to me: "Willem, you do it." Meaning I was to write on the walls of the Dreamer. This is why I was always in trouble in school—Piet and Jan would say, "Willem, you do it," and whatever it was—plugging up the toiletten in the school, or taking air out of the teacher's fietsen . . . bicycles—I would do it. Soo—I took up a can of the paint and in very big letters, I wrote in Dutch that our schoolmaster, Mijnheer Van Doorn, was a gas-passer. Everyone could read the letters from far away. And just as I was finishing this, and Piet and Jan were laughing behind me, I looked—I was on my knees, pressed up against the dyke— and I could see that the wall of the Dreamer was cracking its surface, very fine little lines, like a goose egg when it breaks from within. And I yelled to my friends—Look! And they came a bit closer, and as we looked, right above my head, a little hole began to peck its way through the clay. And there was just a small trickle of water. And Jan said: "Willem, put your thumb in that hole." And by that time, the hole in the dyke was just big enough to put my thumb in. "Why?" I asked of Jan. "Just do it," he said. And so I did. And once I put my thumb in, I could not get it out. Now we could hear the waves crashing. The Sleeper began to collapse. Only the Dreamer remained to hold off the savage water. "Help me!" I yelled to Jan and Piet—but they ran away. "Vlug!" I cried—but no one could hear me. And I stayed there, crouching, with my thumb stuck into the clay. And I thought what if the Dreamer should give in, too. I thought how my body would storm and swirl over the fields. How all the cattle would die. I thought of my maman, and how she would cry, and I tried not to cry, too. I put my shoulder against the clay and felt the pounding, like blood. How young I was to die.

Have you ever prayed for deliverance against all hope? [. . .]

I thought that soon my body would feel nothing, like my thumb. But the Dreamer held. And finally there came wagons with men from the village, holding lanterns and sand and straw. And they found me there, strung up by my thumb, beside the big black letters: Mijnheer Van Doorn is een gaspasser. And they freed me and said I was a hero, and I became the boy who held back the sea with his thumb. [. . .] I was stupid. Wrong place, wrong time.

SIDE MAN

By Warren Leight

One of the sidemen in Warren Leight's elegy to the world of jazz musicians in the 1950s, Jonesy is a trombone player and a junkie ("Not really a junkie junkie. More of an addict. He never misses a gig."). In need of a fix, he "goes to see a man about some horse" and gets arrested. But it's the weekend, and when his friend Gene finally gets into the jail to see him on Monday—the time of this speech—he's been badly beaten by his interrogators.

JONESY: I'm all fucked up, Gene. [. . .] They wanted me to tell them who my dealer was. They said, we'll give you a fix, if you tell us where you cop. They waved it in front of my face. I was dying for it. But I said, I can't trust you guys. Let me fix myself up first, then I'll tell you where I cop. So the bastards give me my stash, they'd already taken half of it for themselves, but I tie off, I shoot up and I'm feeling no pain. OK wise ass, they say, tell us where this heroin comes from? I look them right in the eye and I tell them the truth: . . . General MacArthur. Well, how the hell do you think this stuff gets into the country? Anyway, this fuckin' bull goes nuts. He smacks me across the face. The other guys let him whale on me for a while before they pulled him off. *(Jonesy opens his mouth, shows Gene his teeth)* He broke three of my teeth Gene. *(Starts to cry)* I don't know if I'll ever be able to play.

I AM A MAN

By OyamO

This political drama is based on true events. In Memphis, 1968, two African-American garbage men were crushed to death by their own machinery, leading to a history-making strike of the Memphis Sanitation Workers. Swahili is a young revolutionary—"enraged," in the playwright's words, with "grand illusions of the 'Black Nation.' Full of rhetoric and style, but dangerous." Here, Swahili introduces himself and his teenage comrade Brotha Cinnamon to T. O. Jones, one of the leaders of the strike, who he has been sent to protect.

SWAHILI: They call me Swahili. This is my podna, Brotha Cinnamon. He's the other half of the bodyguard contingent assigned to protect you by Commander Whisper. I know you heard about P. J. Whisper! [. . .]

P. J. Whisper trying to bring knowledge and discipline to the community. He feels the community have the right to defend theyself against enemies by any means necessary. He don't mean no harm to nobody 'bout nothin', just so long as they don't mean no harm to captured Africans in America. That's his whole philosophy in a nutshell. And he got a social program to go 'long wit dat. [. . .]

You represent the only black power move in this city. Everybody else talkin' and walkin' in step to whitey's brass band. You stepped forward and declared yo'self a black man. You a runaway. That's dangerous in Babylon. These crackers fidden ta swoop down on you like a flock of ducks on a fat junebug. You need protection and the Invaders program say protect you at all costs, by any means necessary, even against yo' will if need be. You a asset to the poor, working people. We here to serve and protect you and yo' family from the people who say they're civilized but ack like beasts, even toward one another. We got a squad stationed outside yo' wife home

now. And me and Brotha Cinnamon, we stationed outside yo'
doe. That's it, mzee. *(Saluting)* Power to the people.

THE DARKER FACE OF THE EARTH

By Rita Dove

*In her first full-length play, former U.S. Poet Laureate Rita
Dove recasts the Oedipus story on an antebellum plantation
in South Carolina. Augustus Newcastle, a handsome mulatto
in his twenties, was taken from his mother shortly after his
birth and raised by a sea captain who treated him as his own
son. Well educated and fiercely angry, Augustus has been
brought in chains to the plantation, where he rouses his fellow
slaves with the story of the violent uprising that led to the creation of the Republic of Haiti.*

AUGUSTUS: Did you know there are slaves who set themselves free? [. . .]

> Santo Domingo, San Domingue, Hispaniola—
> three names for an island
> rising like a fortress
> from the waters of the Caribbean.
> An island of sun and forest,
> wild fruit and mosquitoes—
> and slaves, many slaves—half a million.
> Slaves to chop sugar, slaves
> to pick coffee beans, slaves to do
> their French masters' every bidding.
> Then one summer, news came
> from the old country: Revolution!
> Plantation owners broke into a sweat;
> their slaves served cool drinks

while the masters rocked on their verandas,
discussing each outrage:
People marching against the king,
crowds pouring into the streets,
shouting three words: [. . .]
Liberté, Égalité, Fraternité—three words
were all the island masters talked about
that summer, while their slaves
served carefully and listened. [. . .]
Black men meeting in the forest:
Eight days, they whispered,
and we'll be free. For eight days
bonfires flashed in the hills:
Equality. For eight days
tom-toms spoke in the mountains:
Liberty. For eight days
the tom-toms sang: Brothers and sisters.
And on the eighth day, swift as lightning,
the slaves attacked. [. . .]
They came down the mountains to the sound of
    tambourines and conch shells.
With torches they swept onto the plantations,
with the long harvest knives
they chopped white men down
like sugar cane. For three weeks
the flames raged; then the sun
broke through the smoke and shone
upon a new nation, a black nation—
Haiti!

7

"PEOPLE FALL FOR ME,
WHAT THEY THINK IS ME."

AUGUST SNOW

By Reynolds Price

Married only a year, twenty-two-year-old Neal Avery has already begun to drift apart from his wife, Taw. Over the course of the play, he will consider an ultimatum she gives him: recommit to his marriage vows or she will leave him. The author's stage direction for this speech, a direct address to the audience, describes Neal's physical actions as a reflection of his emotional state: "As he speaks he gradually retreats; by the end he is far upstage, marooned."

NEAL: One thing I know I'm not is conceited. So believe what I say, in this one respect. The trouble, my whole life, has been this—people fall for me, what they *think* is me. They mostly call it love, and it generally seems to give them fits. They think life can't go on without me—when I know life can go on in the dark if they blind you, butcher you down to a torso, stake you flat on a rank wet floor and leave you lonesome as the last good soul. Neal Avery can't save the *shrubbery* from pain, much less human beings. It may be the reason I act so bad to Taw and my mother and Porter, my friend. It may be why I'm soaked to the ears so much of the time—*I know I'm me*, an average white boy with all his teeth, not Woodrow Wilson or Baby Jesus or Dr. Pasteur curing rabies with shots.

Who on God's round Earth do they think I am? Who would patch their hearts up and ease their pain? If I stand still here for many years more, won't they wear me away like the

Sphinx or a doorsill, just with the looks from their famished eyes? If I wasn't a Methodist, if this wasn't home, wouldn't I be well advised to strip and run for the nearest desert cave and live among wolves or crows or doves? Wouldn't they simply elect me gamekeeper? Am I ruined past help? Could I take ten steps on my own—here to there—much less flee for life, for my good and theirs?

THE CHEMISTRY OF CHANGE

By Marlane Meyer

Baron is the eldest son of a glamorous and controlling mother, Lee. When the play (which is set in Long Beach, California, in 1955) begins, Lee has just made arrangements to bring him home after six weeks in detox. Now forty, he is a charming, dissolute alcoholic—a serious drunk—although Lee refuses to acknowledge it; she tells people that he has been in the Veteran's Hospital recovering from the war. This speech, the first time we meet Baron, is addressed directly to the audience.

BARON: My mother tells people I have mustard gas poisoning. But that's not true. That's an excuse she's invented because she's ashamed of how I turned out. She's got these archetypes. My brother Farley is a "malingerer." My sister Corlis is "her good right hand." My brother Shep is "sensitive" and I'm a "good-looking drunk." This is how you keep from seeing the truth. She looks at me and sees this archetype. But the truth is, I pass in the world as a monster. Or maybe I should say, minister? My ministry is lost women. Very intelligent, very lost women will find me, like the virgin finds the volcano, and we will begin this conversation that takes us straight to hell; home to hell where we can talk frankly about our mistakes, talk endlessly about what went wrong, all the different ways life has disappointed us. I've cultivated this way of listening to them talk, just the right measure of fascination and detachment. Of course, the truth is that I am not listening at all. I am waiting for my turn to speak, and when I do, I don't shut up. I can make a sentence last for two or three hours. That's the kind of sadist I am. And if the woman tries to interrupt, which she will because she's drunk, I become ENRAGED. And, of course, this is the point. This is what I am saying when I say let's go someplace and have a drink. They think it's the prelude to intimacy. But what I'm really saying is, I need to become enraged, I need to become a monster. Because when I am this monster, I believe that whoever I am with represents the chaos in my life and that if I can fix them, then I myself can become healed. From my perspective I am making a loving gesture. From their perspective I am a vicious nag, an unrelenting scold that will not let them sleep until I have wounded them in ways I myself feel wounded. *(Beat)* You don't know what a comfort it is to pass in the world as a monster.

ZERO POSITIVE

By Harry Kondoleon

Harry Kondoleon describes Patrick, an actor, this way: "Good-looking but banal, one of a million. As he will go mad in this scene, it is important he start with a place to build, gradually becoming furious, making little peaks and valleys of emotional outburst before falling off the top." Immediately before this monologue, Patrick unexpectedly bursts into song—a big musical-comedy style number—in front of his friend Himmer.

PATRICK: My voice teacher can't believe how far along I've come. I'm one of those people who never thought they could sing who really can. It's important to have an audition song at your fingertips you can just leap up and do whenever you have an opportunity. *(Sings suddenly again, peppy)* Took me by surprise! *(Winking)* Just about my size! *(Stopping)* What do you think? [. . .]

I wrote it myself. I figured I didn't want to screw around with copyright and all, you know, if something takes off. [. . .]

It's a very small part, but that's all I go up for these days is very small parts. I'm between age groups. I'm too old to play a teenager and too young to play an old man. And in TV, film and theatre they're very narrow. They admit it, they say they're very narrow. I go to an audition and I'm brilliant, I mean it, *drop-dead brilliant.* I know it, it's not an opinion. My cues are superb. I'm incapable of uttering a false word. I'm tops in emotional guns! A relative of Stella Adler told me she'd never seen physical work like mine. I'm a natural that way. My childhood was very athletic. I fence. I dive. I ski. I can climb ropes. I can shoot a pistol. I can do modern dance. I have an appreciation for the ballet. *Why won't my career take off!*

ANGELS IN AMERICA, PART ONE: MILLENNIUM APPROACHES

By Tony Kushner

Roy is a successful New York lawyer, who is based on Roy M. Cohn, who died in 1986 from an AIDS-complicated illness. According to the author, "The character is based on the late Roy M. Cohn, who was all too real . . . but this Roy is a work of dramatic fiction; his words are my invention, and liberties have been taken." He is the type of aggressive business person who "conducts business with great energy, impatience and sensual abandon: gesticulating, shouting, cajoling, crooning . . ."

Here, Roy is with his doctor, Henry, in Henry's office. Henry has gone over Roy's symptoms—three lesions, swelling of the glands, fungus under his fingernails.

ROY: This is very interesting, Mr. Wizard, but why the fuck are you telling me this? [. . .] This disease . . . [. . .] It afflicts mostly homosexuals and drug addicts. So why are you implying that I . . . *(Pause)* What are you implying Henry? [. . .] I'm not a drug addict. [. . .] What, what, come on Roy what? Do you think I'm a junkie, Henry, do you see tracks? [. . .] Say it. [. . .] Say, "Roy Cohn, you are a . . ." [. . .] "You are a . . ." Go on. Not "Roy Cohn you are a drug fiend." "Roy Marcus Cohn, you are a . . ." Go on, Henry, it starts with an "H." [. . .] *With an "H,"* Henry, and it isn't "Hemophiliac." Come on . . . [. . .] No, say it. I mean it. Say: "Roy Cohn, you are a homosexual." *(Pause)* And I will proceed, systematically, to destroy your reputation and your practice and your career in New York State, Henry. Which you know I can do. [. . .] So say it. [. . .] AIDS.

Your problem, Henry, is that you are hung up on words, on labels, that you believe they mean what they seem to mean. AIDS. Homosexual. Gay. Lesbian. You think these are names that tell you who someone sleeps with, but they don't tell you that. [. . .] No. Like all labels they tell you one thing and one thing only: where does an individual so identified fit in the food chain, in the pecking order? Not ideology, or sexual taste, but something much simpler: clout. Not who I fuck or who fucks me, but who will pick up the phone when I call, who owes me favors. This is what a label refers to. Now to someone who does not understand this, homosexual is what I am because I have sex with men. But really this is wrong. Homosexuals are not men who sleep with other men. Homosexuals are men who in fifteen years of trying cannot get a pissant antidiscrimination bill through City Council. Homosexuals are men who know nobody and who nobody knows. Who have zero clout. Does this sound like me, Henry? [. . .] No. I have clout. A lot. I can pick up this phone, punch fifteen numbers, and you know who will be on the other end in under five minutes, Henry? [. . .] Even better, Henry. His wife. [. . .] I don't want you to be impressed. I want you to understand. This is not sophistry. And this is not hypocrisy. This is reality. I have sex with men. But unlike nearly every other man of whom this is true, I bring the guy I'm screwing to the White House and President Reagan smiles at us and shakes his hand. Because *what* I am is defined entirely by *who* I am. Roy Cohn is not a homosexual. Roy Cohn is a heterosexual man, Henry, who fucks around with guys. [. . .] And what is my diagnosis, Henry? [. . .] No, Henry, no. AIDS is what homosexuals have. I have liver cancer.

8

"PEOPLE I KNOW ARE DYING."

LONELY PLANET

By Steven Dietz

AIDS is never mentioned in Steven Dietz's play, although the author calls his work a "parable and lament" about the subject. More directly, it is a play about friendship, specifically the bond between Jody and Carl, two lonely men living in an anonymous American city. Jody, who is in his forties, owns a map store; he has become fearful and unable to leave it. Here, he confides in the audience about the Greenland Problem, a central metaphor of the play.

JODY: Any talk of maps ultimately comes around to one very specific, lingering issue: The Greenland Problem. *(He indicates a large Mercator Projection World Map on the wall)* Now, you may know this, but Greenland is actually about the size of Mexico. However, on the well-known Mercator projection map—the one hanging in front of your classrooms in grade school—Greenland appears to be roughly the size of South America and twice the size of China. Clearly a world power to be reckoned with, if it were, you know, habitable. The Mercator map also shows most of the earth's land mass to be in what we consider the "north," when, in fact, the "south" is more than double the size of the north. Scandinavia seems to dwarf India, though India is three times as large. And the old Soviet states appear to be twice the size of the entire African continent. In reality they are smaller. Smaller by, oh, about four million square miles.

A map maker takes a messy round world and puts it neat and flat on the wall in front of you. And to do this, a map maker must decide which distortions, which faulty perceptions he can live with—to achieve a map which suits his purposes. He must commit to viewing it only from one angle.

The Mercator map, developed in Germany in 1569, was a great aid to navigators since, for the first time, all lines of longitude ran perpendicular to the equator—or straight up to the top of the map—rather than converging toward the poles. This meant that all the lines of longitude and latitude intersected at right angles—and this meant that, for the *first time*, a sailor could draw a straight line between two fixed points on the map and steer a constant course between them. The map had accounted for the curve of the earth—the sailor did not have to. To accomplish this, Mercator had to accept a distortion: The parallel lines of latitude would have to be spaced progressively further apart as they moved away from the equator. This, in turn, would progressively distort the sizes and shapes of land masses—from zero distortion at the equator, to absolute distortion at the poles . . . the Greenland Problem.

Mercator was a brilliant man. He freed the art of cartography from superstition, from the weight of medieval misconceptions. And his map revolutionized global navigation. He never intended it as a tool to teach the sizes and shapes of countries. He never intended to make Greenland a global behemoth. *(He points at the Mercator map)* But, nearly four hundred and fifty years after Mercator, we still think the earth looks like this. It doesn't. It never has. But we've come to accept the distortion as fact. We've learned to see the world from this angle.

I like this map. I sell this map. I don't warn people when they buy it that, like any good newspaper, it contains a few lies. And I've grown accustomed, when I feel the tug of a perplexed child on my sleeve, to turn and patiently say: "No, it's not really that big."

Maybe it's comforting to us because we, too, have our blind spots. We, too, have things on the periphery of our lives that we distort—in order to best focus on the things in front of us. In order to best navigate through our days. Sometimes, though, these things on the periphery, these things that we do not understand, these *far away* things grow to massive proportions—threatening to dwarf our tiny, ordered, known world. And when they get big enough, we are forced to see them for what they are.

People I know are dying.

This is my Greenland Problem.

LONELY PLANET

By Steven Dietz

Jody and Carl are friends, but Jody has no idea what Carl does for a living. Every day, he tells a different story—each one more colorful and mysterious than the last—about his job. This is the story he tells of being a tabloid reporter.

CARL: No one understands, Jody. They really don't. There are all these so-called "reputable" journalists who walk around bitching and moaning how hard it is to cover the news. How *taxing* it is to look around and put into inverted pyramid form something that happened. I should be so lucky, Jody. So you think I can get away with just typing up stuff that happened? Please. When you write for a tabloid, you have to *create* the news. And believe me, *that* is taxing. Many's the day I wished I could walk out my door, see a little fire across the street, go to work and type it up: "A little fire happened yesterday across the street." How sweet, how simple. But that little fire is not a story at my paper unless an elderly woman with a foreign accent was washing dishes, and she looks down at the white plate she is scrubbing, and there, there on the white plate she is holding is the face of Jesus, Jesus himself, all beatific and covered with suds—and the face of Jesus speaks to her.

The face of Jesus says: "Drop. The. Plate." And the woman is frozen with fear. And again, Jesus says: "Drop. The. Plate." And the woman speaks. The woman says: "It's part of a *set*." Jesus stands firm. "If you want to be with me in heaven, you will drop. The. Plate." The woman is shaking with fear. She tries to explain that it was a wedding gift some forty years ago from an uncle who suffered from polio and died a pauper—but Jesus doesn't give an inch. It's as though he's gone back and read the Old Testament. "I'll give you one more chance," he says, "then I'll have the fire of hell consume your soul." The woman, tears streaming down her face, tries to quickly submerge him under the soapy water—but the water is gone. The sink is gone. Only the plate, and the face, remain. She stares at him, trembling. He says: "Well?" She has a realization. This is not Jesus. This is not her Lord and Savior. This is an *impostor*. This is the spirit of Satan entering the world through her dishware. She looks the plate squarely in the face and says: "I renounce you." Within seconds, she's toast. So is the building. The firemen do not find the slightest trace of her. But there, in the midst of the smoking rubble, the dinner plate shines white and pristine. And burned into it forever is the image of the woman's final, hideous expression. The last face she made before she became a china pattern.

My paper can run a story like that.

THE BALTIMORE WALTZ

By Paula Vogel

Carl is the head librarian of literature and languages at the San Francisco Public Library—"a very important position," his sister Anna tells us. He speaks six languages and desperately wants to go abroad. The Baltimore Waltz, playwright Paula

Vogel writes in an introduction to the play, is "a journey with Carl to a Europe that exists only in the imagination." A commemoration of her own brother (also named Carl) and his death from AIDS, Vogel dedicated the play: "To the memory of Carl—because I cannot sew."

CARL: Good morning, boys and girls. It's Monday morning, and it's time for "Reading Hour with Uncle Carl" once again, here at the North Branch of the San Francisco Public Library. This is going to be a special reading hour. It's my very last reading hour with you. Friday will be my very last day with the San Francisco Public as children's librarian. Why? Do any of you know what a pink slip is? *(Holds up a rectangle of pink paper)* It means I'm going on a paid leave of absence for two weeks. Shelley Bizio, the branch supervisor, has given me my very own pink slip. I got a pink slip because I wear this— *(He points to a pink triangle on his lapel)* A pink triangle. Now, I want you all to take the pink construction paper in front of you, and take your scissors, and cut out pink triangles. There's tape at every table, so you can wear them too! Make some for Mom and Dad, and your brothers and sisters. Very good. Very good, Fabio. Oh, that's a beautiful pink triangle, Tse Heng.

Now before we read our last story together, I thought we might have a sing-along. Your parents can join in, if they'd like to. Oh, don't be shy. Let's do "Put your finger in the air." Remember that one? *(He begins to sing. He also demonstrates)*

"Put your finger in the air, in the air.
Put your finger in the air, in the air.
Put your finger in the air, and wave it everywhere.
Put your finger in the air, in the air.

"Put your finger up your nose, up your nose.
Put your finger up your nose, up your nose.
Put your finger up your nose, and pick whatever grows.
Put your finger up your nose, up your nose."

Third verse! *(He makes a rude gesture with his middle finger)*

"Put your finger up your ass, up your ass.
Put your finger up your ass, up your ass.
Put your finger up your ass, and pass a little gas.
Put your—"

What, Mrs. Bizio? I may leave immediately? I do not have to wait until Friday to collect unemployment? Why, thank you, Mrs. Bizio.

Well, boys and girls, Mrs. Bizio will take over now. Bear with her, she's personality-impaired. I want you to be very good and remember me. I'm leaving for an immediate vacation with my sister on the East Coast, and I'll think of you as I travel. Remember to wear those pink triangles.

THE LIVING

By Anthony Clarvoe

Inspired in part by Daniel Defoe's novel A Journal of the Plague Year *and historical testimony, Anthony Clarvoe's play is set in London during the outbreak of the Black Plague in 1665, when more than one hundred thousand lives were claimed. A metaphorical account of the response to the early years of the AIDS crisis,* The Living *is a tribute to the courage of those who stayed in London to fight the disease—and a damning account of those who fled in fear from the sick and dying. One of the real-life figures whose character and testimony (spoken directly to the audience throughout) appear in the play is Captain John Graunt, a scientist in his thirties, who studies the cycles, trends and statistics that inform the spread of the Plague. As he explains in the first speech of the play, "What we did may be of use to you, if this ever should happen again."*

GRAUNT: And here, I confess it, there is a gap in my account. People ask me, "Did you . . . lose anyone? Did anyone close to you . . ." Die, is what they mean. And that question, that question . . . is not their fault. They weren't there, you see. As I was. They're not . . . here. Always.

Did you lose anyone. Who died.

In the month of June, we lost a thousand people to the plague. In the month of July, we lost a thousand people every week. In the month of August, we lost a thousand people every day. And one day, after all the deaths that had gone before, and with everyone gone from the city who could, with so few of us left alive, one day, toward summer's end, we lost a thousand every hour.

You have to understand: we did not know this at the time. All we knew . . . all we knew was that the sun was very hot. From dawn onwards it was a noontime sun, at a steeper and steeper angle, unblinking, until it stood in the center of the sky and that was all we knew, that the sun was very hot, and there was nowhere we could go and not hear screaming.

I say we lost a thousand every hour, but it was probably more, for that day . . . that was the day we lost count of ourselves. And what we did, what we must have done to be among those still alive by the end of the day, none of us can tell. We became a different species, without the power to speak to you. And then we were human again, but with no words for what we must have done.

On that day, everyone in London died. All of us.

Some of us . . . came back. But with a gap in our accounts.

But this must be part of what I tell you, as your guide to this place, like our cartographers, who, in the places of which no description is possible, can only write: "Here There Be Tygers."

THE LIVING

By Anthony Clarvoe

Set in London during the outbreak of the Black Plague in 1665, The Living *is a metaphorical account of the response to the early years of the AIDS crisis. Captain John Graunt is a real-life figure, a young scientist who studied the spread of the disease, and appears as a character here. In this monologue, addressed to the audience, he reveals the weariness of being a witness to such human suffering.*

GRAUNT: I was visiting the offices of Cripplegate parish, I wanted to check on what I suspected was some terrible underreporting. The office was locked, in the middle of the day, I called, no answer. I found a sexton, we broke in, and there was the parish clerk, at his desk, parish register on his desk, his head on the parish register. [. . .] In the middle of making an entry. I told the sexton to go for a doctor, he said the man was dead, we needed a searcher, I ordered him to go for a doctor, I was very upset, I didn't know why, I hadn't known the man. The sexton went for help, and I stood there, looking. I should have left the room, but I couldn't help looking. [. . .] At the ledger. He'd been underreporting, and now I understood why, he must have been ill, so I wanted to see his numbers. I could see on the open page, almost the last thing he'd written. I was peering around his head. There was ink on his cheek. The entry for plague read five hundred and four. [. . .] I stood there thinking, five hundred and four. Yes, terrible. But. Did he count himself? [. . .] I stood there, thinking that. May I tell you something? You have been so open to my information. [. . .] Yes, so I think it's important that you know this. You see, I have always followed the trends. And death is so much the rage now. Sometimes the plague so infects my mind that I begin to think, all right, perhaps the world would not be worse off, with fewer people. Not excluding myself in this, not by any means. Each of us is a loose end, really, I know what a sinful thought this is. I put it down quickly. But the thought returns. I think of the world as a great equation, a problem whose solution I pursue with too much impatience. So many wretched sufferers, and their suffering children, on and on. Whole groups of people would simplify matters considerably if they would just disappear. I think this! And then I remember how I yearn for people who think like me to govern the world. What if someone like me were in charge of things, and yielded to this thought? I wonder if I'm doing a dangerous thing. I wonder . . . if almost anything can become a plague. I just thought you should keep it in mind. For the future.

9

"THE POINT IS HUSBAND AND WIFE, MAN AND WOMAN, ADAM AND RIB."

THE MARRIAGE OF BETTE AND BOO

By Christopher Durang

In Christopher Durang's black comedy about the emotional reverberations of an unhappy marriage, Bette and Boo are not destined for happiness. Bette, after giving birth to one healthy baby, has delivered four stillborn children; Boo drinks. Father Donnally gives a retreat every year for young married couples in his parish. He invites Bette and Boo, who come with their entire family, including their siblings and parents.

FATHER DONNALLY: Young marrieds have many problems to get used to. For some of them this is the first person of the opposite sex the other has ever known. The husband may not be used to having a woman in his bathroom. The wife may not be used to a strong masculine odor in her boudoir. Or then the wife may not cook well enough. How many marriages have floundered on the rocks of ill-cooked bacon? *(Pauses)* I used to amuse friends by imitating bacon in a saucepan. Would anyone like to see that?

(Father Donnally falls to the ground and does a fairly good—or if not good, at least unabashedly peculiar—imitation of bacon, making sizzling noises and contorting his body to represent becoming crisp. Toward the end, he makes sputtering noises into the air. Then he stands up again. All present applaud with varying degrees of approval or incredulity.)

I also do coffee percolating. *(He does this)* Pt. Pt. Ptptptptptptptptpt. Bacon's better. But things like coffee and bacon are important in a marriage, because they represent things that the wife does to make her husband happy. Or fat. *(Laughs)* The wife cooks the bacon, and the husband brings home the bacon. This is how St. Paul saw marriage, although they probably didn't really eat pork back then, the curing process was not very well worked out in Christ's time, which is why so many of them followed the Jewish dietary laws even though they were Christians. I know I'm glad to be living now when we have cured pork and plumbing and showers rather than back when Christ lived. Many priests say they wish they had lived in Christ's time so they could have met Him; that would, of course, have been very nice, but I'm glad I live now and that I have a shower. [. . .]

Man and wife, as St. Paul saw it. Now the woman should obey her husband, but that's not considered a very modern thought, so I don't even want to talk about it. All right, don't obey your husbands, but if chaos follows, don't blame me. The Tower of Babel as an image of chaos has always fascinated me . . .

[. . .] Now I don't mean to get off the point. The point is husband and wife, man and woman, Adam and rib. I don't want to dwell on the inequality of the sexes because these vary from couple to couple—sometimes the man is stupid, sometimes the woman is stupid, sometimes both are stupid. The point is man and wife are joined in holy matrimony to complete each other, to populate the earth and to glorify God. That's what it's for. That's what life is for. If you're not a priest or a nun, you normally get married. [. . .] Man and wife are helpmates. She helps him, he helps her. In sickness and in health. Anna Karenina should not have left her husband, nor should she have jumped in front of a train. Marriage is not a step to be taken lightly. The Church does not recognize divorce; it does permit it, if you insist for legal purposes, but in the eyes of the Church you are still married and you can never be unmarried, and that's why you can never remarry after a divorce because that would be bigamy and that's a sin and illegal as well. *(Breathes)* So, for God's sake, if you're going to get married, pay attention to what you're doing, have conversations with the person, figure out if you *really* want to live with that person for years and years and years, because you can't change it. Priests have it easier. If I don't like my pastor, I can apply for a transfer. If I don't like a housekeeper, I can get her fired. *(Looks disgruntled)* But a husband and wife are *stuck* together. So know what you're doing when you get married. I get so *sick* of these people coming to me after they're married, and they've just gotten to know one another *after* the ceremony, and they've discovered they have nothing in common and they hate one another. And they want me to come up with a solution. *(Throws up his hands)* What can I do? There is no solution to a problem like that. I can't help them! It puts me in a terrible position. I can't say get a divorce, that's against God's law. I can't say go get some on the side, that's against God's law. I can't say just pretend that you're happy and maybe after a while you won't know the difference because, though that's not against God's law, not that many people know how to do that, and if I suggested it to people, they'd write to the Bishop complaining about me and then he'd transfer me to some godforsaken place in Latin America without a shower, and all because these people don't know what they're doing when they get married. *(Shakes his head)* So I mumble platitudes to these people who come to me with these insoluble problems, and I think to myself, "Why didn't they *think* before they got married? Why does no one ever *think*? Why did God make people stupid?" *(Pause)* Are there any questions?

IN THE BLOOD

By Suzan-Lori Parks

In this modern-day retelling of The Scarlet Letter, *Hester, La Negrita is a single mother with not one but five illegitimate children, and the society that condemns her is contemporary urban America. Chilli, the father of her oldest child, was the one man she truly loved, but he abandoned her fourteen years ago.*

Now Chilli has come back, hoping to rekindle their relationship with a country-and-western song—and a marriage proposal. But Chilli doesn't know about Hester's other four children, who enter halfway through this scene.

Note: the "(Rest)," an aspect of what Parks understatedly calls her use of "slightly unconventional theatrical elements," signifies "a little time, a pause, a breather," a transition for the actor and the character. Bully, Trouble, Beauty and Baby are Hester's other children.

CHILLI:
I want you to look at me. I want you to take me in. Ive been searching for you for weeks now and now Ive found you. I wasnt much when you knew me. When we knew each other I was—I was a shit.
(Rest)
I was a shit, wasn't I? [. . .]
We was young. We had romance. We had a love affair. We was young. We was in love. I was infatuated with narcotics. I got you knocked up then I split. [. . .]
I need time. Time to get to know you again. We need time alone together. [. . .]
Things move fast these days. Ive seen the world Ive made some money Ive made a new name for myself and I have a loveless life. I dont have love in my life. Do you know what thats like? To be alone? Without love? [. . .]
Im looking for a wife. [. . .]

This is real. The feelings I have for you, the feelings you are feeling for me, these are all real. Ive been fighting my feelings for years. With every dollar I made. Every hour I spent. I spent it fighting. Fighting my feelings. Maybe you did the same thing. Maybe you remembered me against yr will, maybe you carried a torch for me against yr better judgment. [. . .]

"Marry me." [. . .]

There are some conditions some things we have to agree on. They dont have anything to do with money. I understand your situation. [. . .]

And your child—ok. *Our* child—ok. These things have to do with you and me. You would be mine and I would be yrs and all that. But I would still retain my rights to my manhood. You understand. [. . .]

I would rule the roost. I would call the shots. The whole roost and every single shot. Ive proven myself as a success. Youve not done that. It only makes sense that I would be in charge. Would you like me to get down on my knees? *(He gets down on his knees, offering her a ring)* Heres an engagement ring. Its rather expensive. With an adjustable band. If I didnt find you I would have had to, well—. Try it on, try it on.

(As Hester fiddles with the ring, Bully and Trouble rush in. Beauty and Baby follow them.) [. . .]

Who do we have here, honey? [. . .]

Who do we have here? [. . .]

Honey? [. . .]

So you all are the neighbors kids, huh? [. . .]

Honey? [. . .]

Im—. I'm thinking this through. I'm thinking this all the way through. And I think—I think—.

(Rest)

(Rest)

I carried around this picture of you. Sad and lonely with our child on yr hip. Struggling to make do. Struggling against all

odds. And triumphant. Triumphant against everything. Like—
hell, like Jesus and Mary. And if they could do it so could my
Hester. My dear Hester. Or so I thought.
(Rest)
But I dont think so.
(Rest)
Im sorry.

THREE DAYS OF RAIN

By Richard Greenberg

*Pip, an actor, is the son of a famous architect. He tells the
audience the story of how his parents met.*

PIP: Hi. Hello. [. . .] My name is Phillip O'Malley Wexler—
well, Pip to those who've known me a little too long. My
father, the architect Theodore Wexler, died of lung cancer at the
age of thirty-eight, even though he was the only one of his generation who never smoked. I was three when it happened, so, of
course, I forgot him instantly. My mother tried to make up for
this by obsessively telling me stories about him, this kind of
rolling epic that trailed me through life, but they, or it, ended
up being mostly about her. Which was probably for the best.

Anyway, it went like this: My mother, Maureen O'Malley
back then, came to New York in the spring of '59. She was
twenty, her parents staked her to a year, and she arrived with a
carefully-thought-out-plan to be amazing at something. Well,
the year went by without much happening and she was miser-
able because she was afraid she was going to have to leave
New York and return, in disgrace, to Brooklyn.

Early one morning, after a night when she couldn't sleep
at all, she started wandering around the city. It was raining,

she had her umbrella, she sat in the rain under her umbrella on a bench in Washington Square Park, and felt sorry for herself. Then she saw my father for the first time.

"There he was," she told me, "this devastatingly handsome man"—that was certainly an exaggeration, he looked like me—and he was obviously, miraculously, even *more* unhappy than she was. He was just thrashing through the rain, pacing and thrashing, until, all at once, he stopped and sank onto the bench beside her. But not because of her. He didn't realize she was there. He didn't have an umbrella so my mother shifted hers over to him.

"Despair," my mother told me, "can be attractive in a young person. Despair in a young person can be seductive."

Well, eventually she got tired of him not noticing the wonderful thing she was doing for him so she said, a little too loudly: "Can I help you? May I be of help to you?" Because he'd been crying. And he jumped! Man, he *shrieked*! But he stayed anyway, and they talked, and I was born, the end.

Okay. So, my mother had been telling me that story for about ten years before it occurred to me to ask: "Why was he crying? What was my father so upset about the first time he met you?" "I never knew," she said. He just told her he was fine, she took him to breakfast, they talked about nothing, and I guess she kind of gawked at him. And the more she gawked, I guess the happier he felt, because by the end of breakfast it was as if nothing had happened and they were laughing and my mother was in love and the worst day of her life had become the best day of her life.

When she first came to New York, my mother would stay up till dawn debating Abstract Expressionism and *Krapp's Last Tape*, and then she'd sneak out to a matinee of one of those plays you could never remember the plot of where the girl got caught in the rain and had to put on the man's bathrobe and they sort of did a little dance around each other and fell in love. And there wasn't even a single good joke, but my mother would walk out after and the city seemed dizzy with this absolutely random happiness, and that's how she met my father. She's hardly ever home anymore. She travels from city to city. I think she's looking for another park bench, and another wet guy. That's okay. I hope she finds him.

SIGHT UNSEEN

By Donald Margulies

Nick is an architect and Englishman whose "rural, working-class speech finds its way into his university accent, particularly when he's been drinking." Underneath Nick's reticent, taciturn demeanor "lies a probing, tireless investigator . . . I study the past in order to make sense of the present." Or at least that is what he tells Jonathan, the former lover of his wife Patricia, when Jonathan turns up at their isolated farmhouse, after not having seen Patricia for fifteen years. For many years, Nick has lived with "The Jonathan Stories" and with the knowledge that Patricia married him, at least in part, to stay in England. Here, he talks to Jonathan, who is about to sneak back to London in the middle of the night.

NICK: She doesn't sleep with me, you know. [. . .] Not that I was ever her type. There was a certain challenge to be found in that. I thought she would *never*, not with me. She was so . . . *attractive*, you know, so confident, so American. The first time she slept with me I thought it must have been because I was her supervisor. I'm sure that was why. When it happened a second time, well, I didn't know *what* to think; I chose to think there was hope. Yes, I opted for hope. In a moment of uncharacteristic brazenness, I asked her to marry me. She accepted. I don't know why. I have my suspicions. *(A beat)* From time to time, I'll fortify myself with stout and kiss her neck, feel her tit, lay my head there. [. . .] Sometimes she'll let me. She'll even stroke my hair. Once she kissed my head. I wanted to reach up and kiss her mouth, but why get greedy and piss her off? [. . .] Some nights she'd respond—oh, she'd respond, or initiate even—and I would rush into it foolishly, trying not to feel I was somehow being rewarded. I take what I can get; I'm English. *(A beat)* She succumbed to my charms tonight, though. Tonight she acquiesced. Did you hear us? [. . .] It was brilliant.

BALLAD OF YACHIYO

By Philip Kan Gotanda

Hiro Takamura, a potter, is resentful of his failures as an artist and bitter about his unhappy marriage. He seeks temporary escape from both of them through alcohol and other women, but nothing really assuages his frustration or anger. When Yachiyo, a sixteen-year-old girl, is sent to live with him and his wife, Takamura finds new energy; although his relationship with Yachiyo is initially confrontational, an attraction between them gradually develops. In this speech, they have only known each other a few months. Takamura tells Yachiyo about his wife Sumiko and how he sold himself into a loveless marriage.

TAKAMURA: What did she tell you? That she was the poor misunderstood wife? That I was cheating on her behind her back? I never lied to her. Right from the beginning she knew what I was. She knew exactly what she was getting. *(Pause)* She liked me. Why I shall never know. She became infatuated with me. Had to have me. Begged, cajoled her father until—ahh, the father. He was a shrewd, shrewd bastard. He cared little about anything but what he could buy and sell for a profit. And he could do that better than any man I've ever met. Have you down on your knees begging him to stick his hands into your pockets. And he could smell a man's weak spot a mile away. Profit, that's all he cared about. That is, except his daughter. His only child. That was his weak spot. And since his daughter wanted me, he made sure she got me. This old man offered me a proposition. I get a second chance to be the artist, to redeem myself in my family's eyes. In exchange, I marry his daughter and—ahh, here's the catch—I give up my name. *(Pause)* I don't know if I really cared one way or the other at the time. So you see, her father bought me for her. Like a pet dog. And she knew what I was. What she was getting. *(Pause. Unsure whether to reveal more)* We had an agreement. This one was between Sumiko and me. Her father didn't know. I told her I didn't love her. And that she must allow me my freedom. That I would be discreet and never bring her shame. This was my side of the bargain. She agreed. Maybe I am getting a bit careless of late—ever since the old bastard died. I guess you could say I've been celebrating. He'd like me drinking, though. That's the one thing we had in common.

10

"YOU WANT TO BE NICE, OR YOU WANT TO BE EFFECTIVE?"

ANGELS IN AMERICA, PART ONE: MILLENNIUM APPROACHES

By Tony Kushner

Kushner's notes to the play include this disclaimer: "Roy M. Cohn, the character, is based on the late Roy M. Cohn (1927–1986), who was all too real; for the most part the acts attributed to the character Roy, such as his illegal conferences with Judge Kaufman during the trial of Ethel Rosenberg, are to be found in the historical record. But this Roy is a work of dramatic fiction; his words are my invention, and liberties have been taken." Roy is a successful New York lawyer and unofficial power broker; he "conducts business with great energy, impatience and sensual abandon." In this scene, from near the end of the play, Roy is a very sick man, dying of AIDS and determined to secure his place in history. Here, he tells Joe Pitt (Roy's one-time protégé, who has just refused Roy's offer to get him a job at the Justice Department in Washington, D.C., described in Roy's monologue later in the volume) about his greatest accomplishment—helping to send Ethel Rosenberg to the electric chair for treason.

ROY: You know what my greatest accomplishment was, Joe, in my life, what I am able to look back on and be proudest of? And I have helped make Presidents and unmake them and mayors and more goddam judges than anyone in NYC ever— AND several million dollars, tax-free—and what do you think means the most to me?

You ever hear of Ethel Rosenberg? Huh, Joe, huh? [. . .] Yes, yes. You have heard of Ethel Rosenberg. Yes. Maybe you even read about her in the history books.

If it wasn't for me, Joe, Ethel Rosenberg would be alive today, writing some personal-advice column for *Ms.* magazine. She isn't. Because during the trial, Joe, I was on the phone every day, talking with the judge . . . [. . .] Every day, doing what I do best, talking on the telephone, making sure that timid Yid nebbish on the bench did his duty to America, to history. That sweet unprepossessing woman, two kids, boo-hoo-hoo, reminded us all of our little Jewish mamas—she came this close to getting life; I pleaded till I wept to put her in the chair. Me. I did that. I would have fucking pulled the switch if they'd have let me. Why? Because I fucking hate traitors. Because I fucking hate communists. Was it legal? Fuck legal. Am I a nice man? Fuck nice. They say terrible things about me in the *Nation.* Fuck the *Nation.* You want to be Nice, or you want to be Effective? Make the law, or subject to it? Choose. Your wife chose. A week from today, she'll be back. SHE knows how to get what SHE wants. Maybe I ought to send *her* to Washington.

THREE HOTELS

By Jon Robin Baitz

Kenneth Hoyle designed a baby-formula marketing policy in Africa and the rest of the Third World for an international conglomerate—a company that is, in his wife Barbara's words, "a perpetrator of an evil" that sells a product, which has been boycotted by four countries. Kenneth used to work in the Peace Corps; now he has a reputation—particularly with his supervisors, Kroener and Mulcahey—for being good at firing people. With a cigar in hand, he talks to the audience.

HOYLE: Anyhow. This Brit kid who works for us. We're at a party for the London office. Me. My wife, Barbara. Bunch of the guys. And the kid says to me, "Mr. Hoyle, sir," (and you know they're gonna fuck ya when they call you sir) "I must tell you I think that what we are doing in Africa is morally indefensible." Well. I mean. There you are. His wife stands there grinning at me like a mad little Staffordshire terrier and there is my *own* wife, grinning, thrilling. And Kroener and Mulcahey taking it in too.

"Morally indefensible," I say. "How so?" And he sputters like a boiling tuber. "You've got saleswomen dressed up as nuns and *nurses* for God's sake running around *hospitals* in Lagos and Nairobi. You're treating baby formula in the Third World as if it's tonic water, which it is not, though by the time the mothers dilute it and the babies drink it, it may as well be. You've got billboards with *doctors* on them, for Christ's sake, proclaiming 'Iris and Rose is better than breast milk.' And the only reason you're getting away with any of this, Mr. Hoyle, is because you're doing it in a place where white people do not go on holiday. Come on," he says. "Defend *that*."

(Long pause. He smiles.)

At World Headquarters you learn a kind of manufactured thuggishness. It is a sort of currency, if you will. The coin of our realm. It means nothing. Less than nothing. It's totally made up.

I look at the boy. "For years," I begin, "this company was run by uncomplicated men who had a clear goal: make a buck. And with the opening of so many world markets, it's taken these men a while to learn that you can't do business in Togo the same way you do in Elbow Lake, Minnesota." I stop for a moment. "'Cause in Togo, pal, things are different." What I'm doing is, I'm doing my gentleman farmer number. (Someone said poor Georgie Bush might have seen me on PBS, that documentary on corporate accountability, and stolen my style.)

Anyhow, back to the party. I say, "Listen. You and I both know that *you* know that. I can see from your tie that you did your hard time at the London School of Economics, so kiddo, clearly you're bright. Therefore, I'm not gonna stand here and play sandbox ethics with ya, so let me offer you this. *Quit.*" I take a breath. The room, it is glistening; it is limpid. He is beginning to look queasy but I'm not about to let this cocksucker off the hook. And this is where I got Mulcahey and Kroener. "If it's so very morally indefensible sitting here overlooking Green Park with your glass of stout and sausage on a toothpick, well then, this must be your resignation, and happy am I to accept it right here and now. *Sir.*"

Exactly eighteen days later I was made Vice-President in charge of Marketing and Third World Affairs.

TALK RADIO

By Eric Bogosian

Barry Champlain hosts Cleveland's most popular and controversial late-night talk show, Nighttalk, *which is about to go national tomorrow. Barry is full of manic energy and self-assurance, he's also got an edge. Barry encourages his callers to "open your mouth and tell me what we're going to do about the mess this country's in." But near the end of this show, which his producer understatedly calls "unorthodox," Barry holds all calls and starts to address his audience "with mounting anger."*

BARRY: Hold the calls.

I'm here, I'm here every night, I come up here every night. This is my job, this is what I do for a living. I come up here and I do the best I can. I give you the best I can. I can't do better than this. I can't. I'm only a human being up here. I'm not God . . . uh . . . I may not be the most popular guy in the world. That's not the point. I really don't care what you think about me. I mean, who the hell are you anyways? You . . . "audience" . . . You call me up and you try to tell me things about myself . . . You don't know me. You don't know anything about me. You've never seen me . . . You don't know what I look like. You don't know who I am, what I want, what I like, what I don't like in this world. I'm just a voice. A voice in the wilderness . . . And you . . . like a pack of baying wolves descend on me, 'cause you can't stand facing what it is you are and what you've made . . . Yes, the world is a terrible place! Yes, cancer and garbage disposals will get you! Yes, a war is coming. Yes, the world is shot to hell and you're all goners . . . Everything's screwed up and you like it that way, don't you? You're fascinated by the gory details . . . You're mesmerized by your own fear! You revel in floods and car accidents and unstoppable diseases . . . you're happiest when others are in pain! And that's where I come in, isn't it? . . . I'm here to lead you by the hand through the dark forest of your own hatred and anger and humiliation . . . I'm providing a public service! You're so scared! You're like the little child under the covers. You're afraid of the boogie man, but you can't live without him. Your fear, your own lives have become your entertainment! Tomorrow night, millions of people are going to be listening to this show, AND YOU HAVE NOTHING TO TALK ABOUT! Marvelous technology is at our fingertips and instead of reaching up for new heights, we try to see how far down we can go . . . how deep into the muck we can immerse ourselves! What do you wanna talk about? Baseball scores? Your pet? Orgasms? You're pathetic. I despise each and every one of you . . .You've got nothing. Nothing. Absolutely nothing. No brains. No power. No future. No hope. No god. The only thing you believe in is me. What are you if you don't have me? I'm not afraid, see. I come up here every night and I make my case, I make my point . . . I say what I believe in. I have to, I have no choice. You frighten me! I come up here every night and I tear into you, I abuse you, I insult you . . . and you just keep calling. Why do you keep coming back, what's wrong with you? I don't want to hear anymore, I've had enough. Stop talking. Don't call anymore! Go away! Bunch of yellow-bellied, spineless, bigoted, quivering, drunken, insomniatic, paranoid, disgusting, perverted, voyeuristic little obscene phone callers. That's what you are. Well to hell with ya . . . I don't need your fear and your stupidity. You don't get it . . . It's wasted on you. Pearls before swine . . . *(Catches his breath)* If one person out there has any idea what I'm talking about . . . *(Suddenly starts taking callers again)* Fred, you're on!

SANTOS & SANTOS

By Octavio Solis

A Federal District Court Judge from San Antonio, Judge Benton is, in the words of another character, "An overfed country club judge . . . heading for the Big Court." Ambitious, opportunistic and right wing, Benton is cultivating minority support in his bid for a seat on the Supreme Court. In this speech, the first time we meet him in the play, he orates at a banquet honoring Miguel and Fernando Santos, Chicano attorneys from El Paso. Tomas (Thomas), the third Santos brother, is an idealistic attorney on whose loyalty the plot— and the Judge's fate—will eventually turn. Benton's seamless transitions between his speech and his true feelings for the Santos brothers are part of the playwright's intention to "defy the physics of what is expected" in his writing.

JUDGE: These boys, these boys, these incorrigible boys. Proud, first-generation American scions of an immigrant cabinetmaker, an importer of furniture, the brothers of the law firm of Santos & Santos blah blah blah
blah
blah

blah

blah blood stewing on my tongue for lying like a sumbitch with his hands on his balls, perjuring myself for miguel and fernando stinkos, two of

the most

invidious,

corrupt,

treacherous,

racketeering

by god the finest attorneys in this state's legal fandangos. In a few short years they have made their firm among the most honored

blah

blah

blah

blah

blasphemy that's what this is but for politics' sake the show must go on but whoa whoa dogie, this boy, this new one, i know from san diego, good son, good skin, good eyes, indeed a santo to behold, but my tribute diarrhears its ugly head

again

again

again I say these turks have won many admirable and deserving judgments at the highest levels of the Texas court, and even in my docket, they have a spectacular reputation for success

blah

blah

blah

black eyes black hair this thomas has a whoreson look to him, abandonment, a look which judges me, by what right, no right, i am a good man, i love my wife and daughter, i stand by the immutable laws of this land, i'm a populist, i voted for lbj, i'm an intellectual, i voted for Nixon, but this young man has a mission

but

but

but it's in the community that they have distinguished themselves, providing scholarships to high-school students blah
blah
blah
blah
blandly how he looks at me, like all mexicans look, with dull
opaque eyes into my heart, where a fear is beshat and a deep
anathema, sing the national anathema, jose can you see, from
the halls of montezuma, we will fight and be
free
free
free free law clinics at the community college, substantial in-
kind services to needy groups
blah
blah
blah
set an example for all people in the Sun City
blah blah
blah blah
blah
latino constituents blah blah blah
blast this golden litigator who cannot transcend the political
reality which is to suck up to this mob for the cameras which
is to testify on behalf of these scalawags which is to sit upon
my bench till the president appoints me to the supremes,
where I will shimmy to the constitution shakedown, political
reality is neither political nor real, but this santos runt, this
beautiful boy, he pierces my soul with a message deep dark
and
bla—
blah
blah
blah
my great privilege to present this plaque to Miguel and
Fernando Santos, Attorneys at Law, on behalf of the El Paso
LULAC Council. For exemplary service to the community.

11

"I AM A MAN OF THE PEOPLE . . ."

IN THE BLOOD

By Suzan-Lori Parks

Suzan-Lori Parks gives each of the adult characters in her modern-day riff on The Scarlet Letter *"confessions," interior monologues that are shared with the audience (see Chilli's monologue in Chapter 2).*

The Doctor, a father to one of Hester's five illegitimate children, works from a roadside "office" and carries all of his paraphernalia (his doctor's shingle and instruments) on his back. He also wears a sandwich board—an eye exam chart— on which the letters spell SPAY.

Note: the "(Rest)," an aspect of what Parks understatedly calls her use of "slightly unconventional theatrical elements," signifies "a little time, a pause, a breather," a transition for the actor and the character.

THE DOCTOR:
>Times are tough:
>What can we do?
>When I see a woman begging on the streets I guess I could
>bring her in my house
>sit her at my table
>make her a member of my family, sure.
>But there are thousands and thousands of them
>and my house cant hold them all.
>Maybe we should all take in just one.
>Except they wouldnt really fit.

They wouldnt really fit in with us.
Theres such a gulf between us. What can we do?
I am a man of the people, from way back my streetside
    practice
is a testament to that
so dont get me wrong
do not for a moment think I am one of those people
    haters who does not understand who does not
    experience—compassion.
(Rest)
Shes been one of my neediest cases for several years now.
What can I do?
Each time she comes to me
looking more and more forlorn
and more and more in need
of affection.
At first I wouldnt touch her without gloves on, but then—
(Rest)
we did it once
in that alley there,
she was
phenomenal.
(Rest)
I was
lonesome and
she gave herself to me in a way that I had never
    experienced
even with women Ive paid
she was, like she was giving me something that was not
    hers to give me but something that was mine
that I'd lent her
and she was returning it to me.
Sucked me off for what seemed like hours
but I was very insistent. And held back
and she understood that I wanted her in the traditional
    way.

And she was very giving very motherly very obliging
   very understanding
very phenomenal.
Let me cumm inside her. Like I needed to.
What could I do?
I couldn't help it.

IN THE BLOOD

By Suzan-Lori Parks

*In this monologue, another confession like the one above, we
see the elements that Parks has characterized as endemic to her
work: "sex, love, violence, history and ritual, all connected."
Hester, destitute and desperate, places most of her hopes (for
money, not love) on Reverend D., who promises to take up a
collection for her among his congregation—but only if she
keeps quiet about his being the father of one of her five children. (See previous speech for a note about the "(Rest).")*

REVEREND D.:
   Suffering is an enormous turn-on.
   (Rest)
   She had four kids and she came to me asking me what
      to do.
   She had a look in her eye that invites liaisons
   eyes that say red spandex.
   She had four children four fatherless children four
      fatherless mouths to feed
   fatherless mouths fatherless mouths.
   Add insult to injury was what I was thinking.
   There was a certain animal magnetism between us.
   And She threw herself at me

like a baseball in the Minors
fast but not deadly
I coulda stepped aside but.
God made her
and her fatherless mouths.
(Rest)
I was lying in the never ending gutter of the street of
    the world.
You can crawl along it forever and never crawl out
praying for God to take my life
you can take it God
you can take my life back
you can have it
before I hurt myself somebody
before I do a damage that I cannot undo
before I do a crime that I can never pay for
In the never ending blistering heat
of the never ending gutter of the world
my skin hot against the pavement
but lying there I knew
that I had never hurt anybody in my life.
(Rest)
(Rest)
She was one of the multitude. She did not stand out.
(Rest)
The intercourse was not memorable.
And when she told me of her *predicament*
I gave her enough money to take care of it.
(Rest)
In all my days in the gutter I have never hurt anyone.
I never held hate for anyone.
And now the hate I have for her
and her hunger
and the *hate* I have for her hunger.
God made me.
God pulled me up.

Now God, through her, wants to drag me down
and sit me at the table
at the head of the table of her fatherless house.

THE SPEED OF DARKNESS

By Steve Tesich

*Lou, a Vietnam veteran, is unable to let go of the war. Dressed
"like a typical homeless tramp . . . carrying his belongings," he
shows up on the doorstep of his old friend Joe, a fellow veteran he has not seen for eighteen years. Lou spends most of his
time moving around the country, following a traveling
Vietnam memorial—what he calls the "Son of the Wall," or
his own "farewell tour of duty." Joe, on the other hand, has
gone on to have a family and become a successful businessman; he has just been named South Dakota's Man of the Year.
His award in hand, he calls his old war buddy a "bum,"
inspiring Lou's discourse on the relationship between urban
homelessness and modern art.*

LOU: I don't want to take anything away from your award,
but I think I've seen a two-story-high version of this very thing
in some industrial park somewhere. There's a term for you.
Industrial park. Talk about your mind-boggling concepts. It's
a curious thing about the homeless . . . *Bums*. Most of us,
I would say ninety-nine percent of us homeless . . . *Bums*, or
at least ninety-nine percent of those homeless *bums* I've
encountered are very conservative when it comes to urban art.
An example. There's a world's biggest Picasso in Chicago and
the last time I passed through there, there wasn't one . . . *bum*
sleeping under it or next to it or even in the vicinity of it. Same
is true for all the other modern-art "pieces" I believe they're

called in all the other cities I've visited. And yet, your traditional statues in the same cities . . . General Grant, Giueseppe Verdi, Simon Bolivar, quite crowded all of them with assorted homeless *bums* sleeping around the pedestals. Pigeons, I've noticed, also seem to prefer the traditional over the modern. The only exception to this whole theory is Henry Moore. Both the birds and the . . . *bums* seem to feel at home with Henry Moore's work. It begs a fuller explanation but I don't have one. It just seems to be so. I remember falling asleep in some park and seeing the moon rise through one of those holes in one of Henry's statues. Perhaps, although I'm not sure, but perhaps, when all is said and done, it's the plaques that are the big difference. Most of your modern urban artists of today eschew plaques. Eschew? Yes, that's right. They just put up something and can't be bothered with letting you know what the hell it is. Not so with your traditional works. It's not much, but it's nice, you know, to have a little reading material before bedtime. A nice plaque. Simon Bolivar, 1783–1830. Liberator of Chile, Bolivia and so forth. You pick up a little history that way. Can't hurt. And then there's the nagging question of an address. Even though one is a homeless *bum* with no permanent address, it's still kind of nice to spend a night with a plaque over one's head. And if you run into old friends on the street during the day and want to get together with them later on that night, you can tell them where you're staying without spending half an hour trying to describe some modern-art "piece" that looks like this or that but not really and doesn't even have a goddamn plaque to tell you what it is. If God, the Creator, had been a modern artist, we wouldn't know what to call anything in the world today because nothing would have a name because God, although inspired during creation, in the end had no idea what it was he had made. Gee, I don't know what to call it. I hate to be pinned down. I mean I can just see Moses coming down the mountain with these post-something modern-art tablets in his hands. Not a word on them, but very conceptual. Here you go, children of Israel. Live according to this. Don't get me wrong. I don't have anything against modern art just because it's modern or post-something or other, I'm just saying it's tough to get a good night's sleep next to one.

12

"THE MOST PRECIOUS ASSET IN LIFE . . . IS THE ABILITY TO BE A GOOD SON."

ANGELS IN AMERICA, PART ONE: MILLENNIUM APPROACHES

By Tony Kushner

Roy is a successful, aggressive, New York lawyer, who is based on Roy M. Cohn, who died in 1986 from an AIDS-complicated illness. But, according to Kushner, "This Roy is a work of dramatic fiction; his words are my invention, and liberties have been taken."

In this scene, Roy attempts to convince his younger protégé Joe Pitt to leave New York and take a job in Washington, D.C., in the Justice Department. (Later, we will learn Cohn wants a "well-placed friend" to intervene in disbarment hearings being brought against him because he "borrowed half a million from one of his clients . . . and forgot to return it.")

ROY: Everyone who makes it in this world makes it because somebody older and more powerful takes an interest. The most precious asset in life, I think, is the ability to be a good son. You have that, Joe. Somebody who can be a good son to a father who pushes them farther than they would otherwise go. I've had many fathers, I owe my life to them, powerful, powerful men. Joe McCarthy most of all. He valued me because I am a good lawyer, but he loved me because I was and am a good son. He was a very difficult man, very guarded and cagey; I brought out something tender in him. He would have died for me. And me for him. Does this embarrass you? [. . .] Well sometimes that's the way. Then you have to find other fathers, substitutes, I don't know. The father-son relationship is central to life. Women are for birth, beginning, but the father is continuance. The son offers the father his life as a vessel for carrying forth his father's dream. Your father's living? [. . .] He was . . . what? A difficult man? [. . .] But he loved you. [. . .] No, no, Joe, he did, I know this. Sometimes a father's love has to be very, very hard, unfair even, cold to make his son grow strong in a world like this. This isn't a good world. [. . .] How long have we known each other? [. . .] Right. A long time. I feel close to you, Joe. Do I advise you well? [. . .] I want to be family. Familia, as my Italian friends call it. La Familia. A lovely word. It's important for me to help you, like I was helped. [. . .]

I'm dying, Joe. Cancer. [. . .]

Please, let me finish. Few people know this and I'm telling you this only because . . . . I'm not afraid of death. What can death bring that I haven't faced? I've lived; life is the worst. Listen to me, I'm a philosopher.

Joe. You must do this. You must must must. Love; that's a trap. Responsibility, that's a trap too. Like a father to a son I tell you this: Life is full of horror; nobody escapes, nobody; save yourself. Whatever pulls on you, whatever needs from you, threatens you. Don't be afraid; people are so afraid; don't be afraid to live in the raw wind, naked, alone . . . Learn at least this: What you are capable of. Let nothing stand in your way.

SIGHT UNSEEN

By Donald Margulies

Known for work that is provocative and enormously popular, artist Jonathan Waxman has "earned both accolades and admonishment." When an article about him appeared on the cover of the New York Times Magazine *("Jonathan Waxman—*

*Bad Boy or Visionary?"), Jonathan thought his father would
be proud, but the story instead bewildered and alienated
him—"How could he have produced a 'visionary'?" Now, a
retrospective of his work in London has brought Jonathan
back into contact with Patricia, his former lover, who he has
not seen since abruptly breaking up with her fifteen years earlier. This scene takes place less than a week after his father's
death.*

JONATHAN: I went to pack up his house the other day? My
parents' house? All his clothes, my old room, my mother's
sewing machine, all those rooms of furniture. Strange being in
a place where no one lives anymore. [. . .] Anyway, what I found
was, he'd taken all the family pictures, everything that was in
albums, shoved in drawers—hundreds of them—and covered
an entire wall with them, floor to ceiling, side to side. I first
saw it years ago, when he'd started. It was his Sistine Chapel;
it took him years. He took my hand (I'll never forget this) he
took my hand—he was beaming: "*You're* an artist," he said to
me, "*you'll* appreciate this." He was so proud of himself
I thought I was gonna cry. Proud and also in a strange way
competitive? [. . .]
    So, there was this wall. The Waxman family through the
ages. Black and white, sepia, Kodachrome. My great-grand-
parents in the shtetl, my brother's baby pictures on top of my
parents' courtship, me at my bar mitzvah. Well, it was kind of
breathtaking. I mean, the sweep of it, it really was kind of
beautiful. I came closer to examine it—I wanted to see how
he'd gotten them all up there—and then I saw the staples. [. . .]
Staples! Tearing through the faces and the bodies. "Look what
you've done," I wanted to say, "How could you be so thought-
less? You've ruined everything!" But of course I didn't say
that. How could I? He was like a little boy. Beaming. Instead
I said, "Dad! What a wonderful job!"
    So, there I was alone in his house, pulling staples out of
our family photos. These documents that showed where I came

from. Did they *mean* anything to him at all? I mean as arti-
facts, as proof of a former civilization, when my mother was
vibrant and he was young and strong and we were a family?
That's all gone now, Patty. It's all gone.

LLOYD'S PRAYER

By Kevin Kling

*Bob, a boy who was raised by raccoons, is high in a tree talk-
ing to his shadow. This is the first speech of the play.*
    *Note: Lloyd, who we will meet later, is a hustler and a
con man posing as an evangelical revivalist.*

BOB: Hello . . . Hello. Don't be afraid. I'm not. Are you new
here? I said are you new here. I'm not. This used to be my
home but it seems different now. Smaller. I don't seem to fit
anymore. What's your name. What are you then. *(He chatters
like a raccoon)* I wish I could speak to you but I've forgotten
how. I have been called many things in my life but I prefer
Bob. I am an orphan. I could no more tell you my real father
than the ingredients in a hot dog. I do remember my mother.
I remember the night she became frozen and died. I remember
snuggling up next to her warm coat, my brothers and sisters
crowding in to get at the milk but I am the biggest so I always
got a spot. At night they all crowded around me because my
coat was the thinnest and didn't keep out the cold. I remember her dark eyes. She taught me to wash my food. She taught
me to never trust a smile because that's right before something
bites. I remember her on the side of the road. She saw the light,
became frozen and died. Lloyd says it happens all the time and
she probably isn't in heaven because she didn't have a south-
ern accent . . . Since I was the biggest my siblings turned to me.
I remember leading them to a house for food, the large cans

full of food the metal trap and the sound of my arm as it broke. I remember pulling to get free. Pulling on the pain. I knew I was human. I knew when I saw the trap. I was not a raccoon. I knew when I put in my arm. I know what I am doing. I am making a choice. I see the trap. I see the choice. I am human I am human. I was trapped, I was human, my arm was broken and a man was running toward me with a gun. Lucky for me he was a doctor.

13

"A FATHER'S LOVE IS A FAIRLY SPECTACULAR THING."

AN ALMOST HOLY PICTURE

By Heather McDonald

A lapsed Episcopal minister, now groundskeeper for The Church of the Holy Comforter, Samuel Gentle speaks directly to the audience for the duration of this one-man play, sharing the experiences that shaped his personal idea of God and wrestling with faith and loss. Samuel's daughter Ariel was born with lanugo, a "mysterious and rare disease" in which "a fine, silky hair coats the face and body," a condition he describes in this excerpted monologue.

SAMUEL: For many years, my wife Miriam and I tried to conceive a child. We lost three babies, a trinity of miscarriages. After the third, we met with our doctor for a lengthy examination and consultation. This doctor was not obviously callous, but he was young and the way he held his head suggested to me he had not yet known grief. His was a confident carriage. The walls of his office assured us of a prestigious education and the prominently displayed photograph of a young wife and two children—a boy and a girl—with lovely teeth, let us know that his practice was not built solely on theories and facts he'd gleaned from textbooks. He was, in addition to his other accomplishments, a family man.

During the examination, I waited for my wife in an outer room. When she was done, Miriam stepped unevenly into the room wearing only one high-heeled shoe and carrying her underwear in her hand. And she said to me with a little, completely uncharacteristic laugh, "Well, Samuel, I am, what one would call, a habitual aborter." [. . .]

Two years later, at the age of forty-two, Miriam gave birth to a tiny girl child covered all over in a white-gold swirl of hair. The doctor (another one) [. . .] held her high and said, "Lanugo." Lanugo? I'd only ever heard this word in relation to the garden. There is a climbing plant, a native to China, called *Clematis lanuginosa*. It's a dark green vine, and the under surface of the leaf is covered with the softest gray wool. What did this have to do with my daughter?

When I suggested we call her Ariel since she seemed to me a tiny, shimmering angel, Miriam snorted (she does that sometimes—snorts) and said, "Humph, a misguided angel."

When I looked at this wrinkled cooing bird that was my daughter and held her tight little fists in my hands, my ribcage expanded to make room as my heart grew bigger. Her whole body shuddered with an intake of breath. A breath of heaven. And what I felt then was truer than what, for most of us, passes for love, because it was uncorrupted by love's hunger and fear of loss and damaging desperation. It was wide open and as big as all creation.

AN ALMOST HOLY PICTURE

By Heather McDonald

Samuel Gentle's daughter Ariel was born with a rare disease (described in the previous monologue) in which fine, silky hair coats her entire body. Here, he shares the effect that this "mysterious affliction" had on his wife Miriam after Ariel's birth.

SAMUEL: When Miriam and I brought Ariel home from the hospital, Miriam handed Ariel over to me, tied her hair in a kerchief, put on an old housedress, and embarked on a whirling attempt at spring cleaning. The kerchief gave her a clownish air like Lucy Ricardo. Only seven days had passed since giving birth, yet unassisted, Miriam dragged all the dining room and living room furniture into the hallway. She varnished and buffed the floors until you could see a reflection. She whacked at cobwebs with a broom wrapped in a dishtowel. She scrubbed dishes and pots already clean, yanking them from their cupboards and scouring them in a great white enamel tub on the kitchen table.

I read Ariel *Goodnight Moon* and *Worms Wiggle*. [. . .] I held Ariel aloft giving her the gift of flight, offering her this view of the world from a bird's vantage. She was open-mouthed, taking in the gentle rush of air. Soaring, her arms stretched wide like some memory of wings. [. . .] She looked down at me, her face shining from the light reflected off my glasses. Her tiny hand reached down touching my cheek. I smiled at my hairy airborne daughter, and she smiled back with sighs too deep for words. After all, a father's love is a fairly spectacular thing. [. . .]

At six o'clock Miriam charged into the kitchen and not long after produced a dinner. We sat down to eat (in the hallway) she still wearing the kerchief and housedress. I said, "Oh, Loooocy," hoping for an, "Oh, Ricky," in response, but I don't think she made the connection.

I looked over at Ariel lying in the bassinet like a sleeping pup. I looked at my daughter's hairiness, and something came over me. Something I had never felt before. I suppose that is part of the bargain of marriage; sometimes you get *turned* on because you happen to be the person nearest. I can't explain what happened next, but I was shaking with fury and out popped, "The hell with you! The hell with you!" Miriam looked startled. I went on, "These pork chops are dry. You have never once in our entire marriage cooked a decent pork chop and I hate you for it. I hate you. I hate you."

Miriam ran from the hallway. I stood, still shaking when she thundered back into the room wailing, "Look, look what you have done to me." She was pointing at her legs. "Every night when you roll over in bed, you slash at my legs with your long toenails you're too selfish to cut for fear of ingrown nails. Selfish! Selfish! I regret the day I ever met you." And with that she ran out. I followed but stopped when I saw three perfect round drops of blood on the floor. I went to my wife who stood in a rage in the middle of her varnished floor staring out a curtainless window and I gathered her up in my arms and I carried her up the stairs and I held her so so close to me and together we wept.

ROOSTERS

By Milcha Sanchez-Scott

Hector's father, Gallo, has neglected his family in his ambition to breed the "ultimate bird," a rooster that he can teach to fight and kill. "You kill your young," Hector says to his father, "and we are so proud of your horrible animal vigor." But Hector, a handsome young man of twenty, has his own ambitions; he wants to escape from the fieldwork he was forced to undertake when his father went to prison. Here, he secretly remembers his first cockfight, which he was taken to by his Abuelo (grandfather).

HECTOR: It was in Jacinto Park . . . the crowd was a monster, made up of individual human beings stuck together by sweat and spittle. Their gaping mouths let out screams, curses, and foul gases, masticating, smacking, eager for the kill. You stood up. The monster roared. Quasimoto, your bird, in one hand. You lifted him high, "Pit!" went the call. "Pit!" roared the monster. And you threw him into the ring . . . soaring with the blades on his heels flashing I heard the mighty rage of his wings and my heart soared with him. He was a whirlwind flashing and slashing like a dark avenging angel then like some distant rainbow star exploding he was hit. The monster crowd inhaled, sucking back their hopes . . . in that vacuum he was pulled down. My heart went down the same dark shaft, my brains slammed against the earth's hard crust . . . my eyes clouded . . . my arteries gushed . . . my lungs collapsed. "Get up," said Abuelo, "up here with me, and you will see a miracle." You, Father, picked up Quasimoto, a lifeless pile of bloody feathers, holding his head oh so gently, you closed your eyes, and like a great wave receding, you drew a breath that came from deep within your ocean floor. I heard the stones rumble, the mountains shift, the topsoil move, and as your breath slammed on the beaches, Quasimoto sputtered back to life. Oh Papi, breathe on me.

LLOYD'S PRAYER

By Kevin Kling

Lloyd is a hustler and a con man; Bob is a boy who was raised by raccoons. Lloyd has made a living off of Bob, whom he calls "stepchild," first exhibiting him as a freak in a sideshow and then using him as an evangelical prop in a religious "crusade." Together, Lloyd and Bob form the unlikely heart of Kevin Kling's satirical black comedy about revival meetings and divine intervention. Immediately preceding this speech, they saw "a terrible sight"—a wall of bugs, a wall of fire and a wall of blood—which was followed by a visitation from the angel of the Lord.

LLOYD: Whiskey. Stepchild give me that bottle. I never seen anything so horrific in all my born days. Wall of fire. Bugs. Blood. I mean blood. I'm not talking a prickly finger-poke, a wall of blood. And . . . I don't even know what that other wall was but the smell . . . augh . . . Lordy Lord . . . My barf glands were busting out all over. Heavens and earth stepchild give me that bottle, can't you see I'm suffering. *(He drinks the whole bottle)* Sorry stepchild but there was barely enough for me. Drink has dug more graves, wrecked more manhood, dishonored more womanhood, broken more hearts, sold more homes, snapped more wedding rings, armed more villains and dethroned more reason than any other poisonous scourge to hit the modern-day world. But it sure takes the edge off. Now what are you looking at. Don't look at me like that. What, you think I had something to do with that mess don't you. I know you do. Well it isn't me bringing on the horrors my furry friend. It looks like you've been found out. That's right stepchild. They're on to . . . you. I tried, you've seen me try to save you. What more can I do? Every day I preach my heart out and look at you. I mean . . . look at you . . . look at you . . . What are you looking at. I'll tell you what you're looking at. A failure. One big fat failure looking at another. What am I gonna do with you. I can't take care of you forever. What am I? A goddamn saint? Not hardly. As of tomorrow we're through. Got me. I gotta let you go. That's it. Final. Don't look at me like that boy, it's not gonna do you any good. You're better off on your own. Better off in the wild where you belong. God, look at you. You are really something you little fur-bearing gold mine. It's a crying shame to get run outta business like this. I tried. I took the test and failed. Took the . . . test . . . the test. That's what He's doing. Of course, He's testing me. How could I be so blind but now I see. It's a simple test of faith and now it's over. I can't quit on you now boy. No sirree. Nice try up there Lord but I'm onto you now. Don't you worry I'm not giving up on the lad. Not with money burning holes in the pockets of countless sinners. Stepchild? Stepchild. Look at me when I'm talking to you boy. Tomorrow we're gonna be right back on that street like we never missed a beat. I'm gonna preach like I never did and you just watch those pockets empty. I am renewed. Now hit that light stepchild. I'm starting to feel the effects of that bottle.

THE YOUNG MAN FROM ATLANTA

By Horton Foote

Houston, 1950. Will Kidder, sixty-four, is "a hearty, burly man with lots of vitality" who wants only the biggest and the best in his life—the best house, the best job, the best doctor. But Will's happiness masks a deeper sorrow. A year earlier, his son died, a probable suicide; the reason why remains a mystery, as Will explains to Tom, his colleague and close friend.

Note: Will is married to Lily Dale; both characters figure prominently in Horton Foote's nine-play "Orphans Home Cycle." This work, which received the Pulitzer Prize, is not included in the cycle.

WILL: It doesn't seem possible he's not here any longer. He was fine young man. One of the best. We weren't anything at all alike you know. [. . .] No, nothing. I'm crazy about sports. He never cared for them. Not that he was artistic like his mother. He wasn't. He had a fine math mind. He was a whiz at math. And he loved school. He was never happier than when he was studying. I thought he was going to stay in college forever. Cost me a fortune. And then the war came along. He was twenty-nine and he volunteered first thing. Couldn't wait to be drafted. Volunteered for the Air Force. He was a bombardier. Came home without a scratch. Made I don't know how many bombing raids and didn't even get a scratch. I thought my boy has a charmed life for sure. When the war was over I wanted to bring him here in the business, but he would have none of it. He got a job in Atlanta. Why Atlanta, I said. You were born and raised in Houston, Texas, the finest city in the whole of the world. I never could figure out exactly what his job was. I don't think he used any of his math skills as far as I could tell. He traveled a lot. He was on a trip for his company that day— *(A pause)* I still can't believe it. [. . .] No. It does me good to talk about it. I can't talk to my wife about it. *(A pause)* He was in Florida for his company and he stopped at this lake to go for a swim. He couldn't swim. Never learned and I never remember hearing of him going swimming before. Anyway, that's what he did this day. This man that owned the lake was there alone and he said it never occurred to him to ask him if he could swim. He said he went into the bathhouse and changed his clothes and came out and waved to him as he walked into the lake. He said he just kept walking until he was out of sight. The man got concerned when he couldn't see him any longer and he yelled to him and when he got no answer he got his boat and rowed out to where he had last seen him and found his body. He had drowned. He was thirty-seven—thirty-seven. Drowned. Our only child. I wanted to have more, but my wife had such a difficult time when he was born that we never had any more. [. . .]

It was the middle of the day. Why in the middle of the day in a lake in Florida out in deep, deep water if you can't swim. *(A pause)* Everyone has their theories, and I appreciate their theories, but I'm a realist. I don't need theories. I know what happened. He committed suicide. Why I don't know.

14

"YOU EVER KILLED ANYBODY?
EVER WANT TO?"

THE INCREDIBLY FAMOUS WILLY RIVERS

By Stephen Metcalfe

Willy Rivers, a rock-and-roll star, became "incredibly famous" when a crazed fan tried to assassinate him during one of his concerts. No longer able to play the guitar the way he used to, Willy is now trying to make a comeback, and goes to meet with the man who shot him. Willy wants to know why the Prisoner, a man he does not know, wanted to kill him, so he visits him in a psychiatric ward. This is the response.

PRISONER: Now we're friends. I have watched you play so many times. [. . .] Oh, yes. In my opinion, you're an artist. You always have been. Like me. [. . .] An artist changes one's perception of reality. I changed yours a lot. [. . .] Don't thank me. At the time, changing your perception of reality wasn't my intention. [. . .] I was trying to kill you. *(Pause)* However, since death might be considered a drastic change in perception, I guess you could say my intentions have been consistent from the beginning. Artistically speaking. [. . .]

You ever killed anybody? [. . .] Ever want to? [. . .] I bet you have. It's great. You're so in control. Of course I'm talking premeditated. You're so . . . powerful. You walk down the street and no one knows how powerful you are. You're like God. All you have to do is act and everything changes. You've taken a color out of a painting and substituted one of your own. You've given somebody else's melody different notes.

You're a pebble that's been dropped in a pond. Concentric circles get wider and wider. [. . .] When you're capable of killing, you're not afraid of anyone! You laugh inside 'cause you know that hardly anybody is capable of striking out the way you are. For keeps. [. . .]

You look good. People like you. Girls, I bet, like you. I bet they want to fuck you. I bet you have fun. I don't have fun. I never did. Why you. Why not me. Why not me!? [. . .] I was contemplating the President but it didn't look like he'd be passing through town for quite some time. You were elected. *(He giggles)* I made a pun. I did, I made a pun, huh!? [. . .] If you must know, it was nothing personal. When I pulled the trigger I wasn't even thinking of you. No. I was thinking of me. I was thinking of me and what everybody else was gonna be thinking of me.

IN THE HEART OF AMERICA

By Naomi Wallace

Boxler is one of the ghost characters that literally haunt this Gulf War drama about homophobia and racism within the U.S. military. The spirit of a soldier who fought in Vietnam, he was part of an American unit that "attacked an undefended village on the coast of central Vietnam . . . and murdered approximately five hundred old men, women and children." By the time he went to trial, however, he was treated as a hero. Holding a black box, he speaks directly to the audience.

BOXLER: Trust me. I'm the man with the box. The Amnesty box. And this time I'm in . . . Iraq. Is that right? *(Beat)* This box you see before you is a very special box. It's a common device we use here within the military, a receptacle in which soldiers can relieve themselves of contraband, no questions asked. Would you like to drop something in it? You can't take those bits and pieces home with you. No, no, no. I've already made the rounds with the other troops. You're not alone. *(Lifts the lid just a bit but then slams it shut)* What distinguishes this particular box is its stench. Now some soldiers are more attached to their souvenirs than others; in one instance, a severed arm was discovered on a military flight leaving the base for Chicago. One might assume that someone somewhere would be disciplined for anatomical trophy-hunting but no, not this time. Lucky, lucky. Are you listening? I'm ready for hell but they won't have me and that's where they're wrong. *(Beat)* All that nasty shit, it took place all the time, before I even killed my first one. But they weren't interested then. And then when they were—bingo—there I was. *(Beat)* Yes, I did it. I never denied it.

MARISOL

By José Rivera

At the dawn of the millennium, New York is an apocalyptic battleground. Marisol's Guardian Angel is preparing to leave her in order to lead a group of rebel angels (the Heavenly Hierarchies) in an insurrection against God. Their revolution has spilled down to Earth, where "time is crippled, geography's deformed" and derelicts and skinheads wield machine guns. In the first scene of the play, the Man with Golf Club enters a subway car and threatens Marisol, "shooting" his club like an Uzi. His Angel, too, has abandoned him, as he tells Marisol.

GOLF CLUB: It was the shock that got me. I was so shocked all I could see was pain all around me: little spinning starlights of pain 'cause of the shocking thing my Angel just told me.

You see, she was always *there* for me. I could *count* on her. She was my very own godblessed little angel! My own gift from God! *(No response. The Man makes a move toward Marisol)* But last night she folded her hot silver angelwings under her leather jacket and crawled into the box I occupy on 180th Street in the Bronx. I was sleeping: nothing special walking through my thoughts 'cept the usual panic over my empty stomach, and the wind-chill factor, and how oh how was I ever going to replace my lost Citibank MasterCard? [. . .] She creeped in. Reordering the air. Waking me up with the shock, the bad news that she was gonna *leave me forever . . . Don't you see?* She once stopped Nazi skinheads from setting me on fire in Van Cortlandt Park! Do you get it now, lady?! I live on the street! I'm dead meat without my guardian angel! I'm gonna be *food* . . . a fucking *appetizer* for all the Hitler youth and their cans of *gasoline . . . (The Man lunges at Marisol and rips the newspaper from her)* [. . .] *(Truly worried)* That means you don't have any protection either. Your guardian angel is gonna leave you too. That means in the next *four or five seconds*, I could change the entire course of your life . . . [. . .] *(Calm, almost pitying)* . . . I could fix it so every time you look in the mirror . . . every time you dream . . . or close your eyes in some hopeless logic that closed eyes are a shield against nightmares . . . *you're gonna think you turned into me . . . (The Man swings the club at Marisol's head)*

SEARCH AND DESTROY

By Howard Korder

Ron, a fast-talking drug dealer who is pretending to be a businessman, has agreed to set up a drug deal that will help a neophyte film producer, Martin, and his partner-in-crime, Kim, finance a movie deal in Howard Korder's drama about greed, violence and the American dream. Here, Ron explains to Martin and Kim why he loves New York.

RON: The best. The best. Absofuckingwhatly the best. Last night. Okay. We get there. This is at Shea. We get there. In the limo. I got, I'm with, the, *Carol*, she does the, the, *fuck*, you know, that *ad*, the fitness, amazing bod, amazing bod, fucking amazing bod, and I have, for this occasion, I put aside my very best, lovely lovely blow, for Carol, who, no, I care about very deeply. So, okay, get to Shea, it's fucking *bat* night, everybody with the bats, fifty thousand bat-wielding sociopaths, security is very tight. *I* have a private booth. In the circle. This is through GE, my little addictive exec at GE. So we entree, me and Carol, and my client, I see, has fucked me over, 'cause there's already someone there, you know who, that talk-show guy, he's always got like three drag queens and a Satanist, and he's there with a girl can't be more than fourteen. "Oops." This fucking guy, my *daughter* watches that show. And between us, heavy substance abuser. I ask him to leave. I mean I come to watch a ball game with my good friend Carol and I'm forced to encounter skeevy baby-fucking cokeheads. One thing leads to the other, politeness out the window he comes at me Mets ashtray in his hand. What do I do. [. . .]

I have a bat, I take this bat, I acquaint this individual in the head with this bat. "Badoing." Right, badoing? He doesn't go down. Stands there, walks out the door, comes back two security guards. "Is there a problem here, boys?" "Well sir, this man, bicka bicka bicka." "Yes, I completely understand and here's something for your troubles." [. . .]

How much did I give these good men to resolve our altercation? I gave them one thousand dollars in U.S. currency. And they were very grateful. Mr. Microphone sits down, doesn't speak, doesn't move rest of the night. Moody fucking person. Mets take it, great ball, home with Carol where we romp in the flower of our youth. I win. I dominate. I get all the marbles. And that is why I love New York.

ROOSTERS

By Milcha Sanchez-Scott

Gallo is "a very, very handsome man in his forties. He is wearing a cheap dark suit, with a white open-neck shirt." This is the first speech of Milcha Sanchez-Scott's play, set in the American Southwest, in which the world of cockfighting takes on a metaphorical context—both sensual and violent—for this story of a divided family. At the start of the play, Gallo has just been released from prison, where he was sent after killing a competitor. His great ambition, he explains to the audience here, is to breed and train the "ultimate bird," even if it means neglecting his wife and children.

GALLO: Lord Eagle. Lord Hawk, sainted ones, spirits and winds, Santa Maria Aurora of the Dawn . . . I want no resentment, I want no rancor . . . I had an old red Cuban hen. She was squirrel-tailed and sort of slab-sided and you wouldn't have given her a second look. But she was a queen. She could be thrown with any cock and you would get a hard-kicking stag every time.

I had a vision, of a hard-kicking flyer, the ultimate bird. The Filipinos were the ones with the pedigree Bolinas, the high flyers, but they had no real kick. To see those birds fighting in the air like dark avenging angels . . . well like my father use to say, "Son nobles . . . finos . . ." I figured to mate that old red Cuban. This particular Filipino had the best. A dark burgundy flyer named MacArthur. He wouldn't sell. I began borrowing MacArthur at night, bringing him back before dawn, no one the wiser, but one morning the Filipino's son caught me. He pulled out his blade. I pulled out mine. I was faster. I went up on manslaughter . . . They never caught on . . . thought I was in the henhouse trying to steal their stags . . . It took time—refining, inbreeding, cross-breeding, brother to sister, mother to son, adding power, rapid attack . . . but I think we got him.

15

"WHAT IS IT THAT MAKES A MAN FEEL SORRY?"

PLAYLAND

By Athol Fugard

Playland is a small traveling amusement park encamped on the outskirts of a Karoo town in South Africa. It is New Year's Eve just after the end of the South Africa Border War, a long and bitter struggle that lasted from 1966 to 1989. "Because of its traumatic effect on the South African psyche," Fugard writes in a note, "it is referred to as South Africa's Vietnam." Two strangers, Martinus Zoeloe and Gideon le Roux (a black man and a white man, respectively) spend the evening talking. Each man holds a memory of murder, which they finally reveal to each other here at the end of the play.

Martinus, Playland's watchman, had stabbed a white man and was sentenced to death; he was released only when the dead man's wife corroborated Martinus's defense, which was that her husband had forced Martinus's woman Thandeka, who was their servant, into his bed.

MARTINUS: Listen to me now. I am going to tell you something. When I was sitting in the death cell, waiting, the prison dominee came to visit me. Dominee Badenhorst. He came to me every day with his Bible. He read to me about the Commandments—specially Number Six—Thou Shalt Not Kill. He said to me, "Martinus, you have sinned. You have killed a man. But if you pray and ask God for Forgiveness and he looks into your heart and sees that you are really sorry, then he will forgive you."

Then I said to him, "But I am not sorry."

Then he said, "Then you will go to Hell Martinus."

"I can't help it, Dominee," I said, "then I will go to Hell, but I can't feel sorry."

He wouldn't believe me. "No," he said, "that is not so. You are a good man Martinus. Look deep into your heart. I know you are sorry for what you did."

"Listen Dominee," I said. "I say it to the Jude and now I say it to you also—if I saw that white man tomorrow, I would kill him again. It would make me very very happy to kill him again."

The dominee was very sad and prayed for me. There in the cell, on his knees, he prayed to God to make me feel sorry. But it is no good. I still don't have that feeling. All the years I was in jail, and all the years I sit here by the fire, I ask myself, "What is it that makes a man feel sorry? Why doesn't it happen inside me?" Baas Joppie—he was the prison carpenter, I was his handlanger [helper, right-hand man]—he was sorry. He killed his father and he was sorry for doing it he cried all the times he told me about it. And Jackson Xaba—they hanged him—guilty four times for rape and murder, he told me also he was sorry. But me . . . ?

(He shakes his head) The dominee said that if I looked deep into my heart I would find that feeling. I try. I look inside. When I sit here every night I look inside and I find feelings, strong feelings for other things. When I remember Thandeka and I wonder where she is, I feel a big sadness inside me. Or when I just sit by the fire when it is cold and the tea is hot, that makes me feel good inside. Bread and meat, good! Rain! Rain falling in this dry Karoo—very good! I even find feelings for dead dogs. But for him—Andries Jacobus de Lange, the Deceased, the man I killed—*No!*

PLAYLAND

By Athol Fugard

After ten years fighting in the South African Border War, Gideon le Roux, a white army veteran, is nearly destroyed, consumed by guilt. He is particularly haunted by a battle in which his company ambushed an enemy's unit. On that day, Gideon did the rounds of counting the dead—"twenty-seven of them that we'd blown away to Kingdom Come." He describes to Martinus, a black watchman at the Playland amusement park who he has just met, what happened when his unit came back a few days later to clean up the decomposing bodies.

GIDEON: Me and another chap was detailed to take the bodies and dump them in a big hole. Oh boy! First we had to load them onto the back of the lorry, one by one—we had to wear gloves and masks it was so bad—then we drove over to the hole. When we got there I see this old woman come out of the bush and stand there and watch us. She didn't do anything or say anything—she just stood there watching.

So we back the lorry up to the hole and started . . . He grabs the hand, I grab a leg, drag it to the edge and then . . . into the hole. First you kind of try to do it nicely you know, because after all they was human beings, but by the time you get halfway through you just don't give a damn anymore—it's hot and you're feeling naar [nauseous] so you just chuck them in. All the time I was doing this I had a strange feeling that it reminded me of something, but I couldn't remember what it was. And the old woman was still standing there watching us. I couldn't take it anymore so I started shouting and swearing at her, telling her to go away, and while I was doing that suddenly it came to me, the thing I was trying to remember.

It was the time we was on holiday at Mossel Bay—me and my mom and my dad. I was still just a little outjie [boy] in a khaki broek. Every day me and my dad would take his fishing rod and go down to the rocks. He would put on some bait and throw out and then wait for a big one. My job was to catch him the small fishes in the rock pools for him to use as bait. So one day I catch this lekker [nice] fat little fish and I'm all excited and I start to cut it up and then—*Here*! man, hundreds of little babies jump out of its stomach onto the rock. Just so big . . . *(Indicating with his fingers)* little babies man!—they already has little black dots where their eyes was going to be—jumping around there on the rock. And the mother fish also, with her stomach hanging open where I had cut her, wagging her tail there on the rock. And I looked down at all of this and I knew man, I just knew that what I had done was a terrible sin. Any way you look at it, whether you believe all that stuff about Heaven and Hell and God Almighty or not it makes no difference. What I had done was a sin. You can't do that to a mother and her babies. I don't care what it is, a fish or a dog or another person, it's wrong!

So then what the hell was going on man? There I was on the back of that lorry doing it again. Only this time it was men I was sommer [just, simply] throwing into that hole. Maybe one of them was that woman's son. Maybe I had killed him. That did it. Something just went inside me and it was snot and tears into that face mask like I never cried in my whole life, not even when I was small. I tore off the mask and gloves and got off the lorry and went over to where the old woman had been standing, but she was gone. I ran into the bush to try and find her, I looked and called, but she was gone. That's where they found me the next day. They said I was just walking around in a dwaal [daze].

[. . .] I wanted to tell her about that little boy. I wanted to tell her that he knew what was right and wrong. I don't know what happened to him, what went wrong in his life, but he didn't want to grow up to be a man throwing other men into a hole like rotten cabbages. He didn't want to be me. And when I had told her all that, I was going to ask her for forgiveness . . . but she was gone.

BOBRAUSCHENBERGAMERICA

By Charles L. Mee

Bob, the Pizza Boy is one of many disparate, seemingly uncon-
nected characters in this play, which—inspired by the artist
Robert Rauschenberg—takes the form of a collage of scenes,
images and texts. We meet him for the first time here, late in
the play, when he shows up with a pizza and proceeds to
expound upon the nature of forgiveness. This is something
Bob, a manic-depressive, has thought a lot about since com-
mitting a triple murder—stabbing his sister, husband and their
son. Bob, playwright Charles L. Mee said in an American
Theatre *interview, "reflects that strain of unfathomable vio-*
lence in America. You listen to him speak, and think, This is
weird and funny, and then, This is horrifying, and then you
begin to have sympathy." Here, Bob answers another charac-
ter, Wilson, who has asked if he thinks the "episode" will
become part of his past.

BOB, THE PIZZA BOY: In the first three or four years there
was a couple of nights where I would stay up thinking about
how I did it, you know. And what they said . . . they told me
later there were something like thirty stab wounds in my sister, but uh, I remember distinctly I just cut her throat once.
That was all, you know, and I don't know where the thirty
stab wounds came from. So that might have been some kind
of blackout thing. You know, I was trying to re- re- re- uh, re-
uh, uh, resurrect the uh, the crime—my initial steps, etcetera.
You know, and uh, and uh, I took, as a matter of fact, it came
right out of the, I was starting the New Testament at the time,
matter of fact I'm about the only person you'll ever meet that
went to, to do a triple murder with a Bible in his, in his pocket,
and, and, listening to a radio. I had delusions of grandeur with
the radio. Uh, I had a red shirt on that was symbolic of, of
some lines in Revelation in the, in the New Testament. Uh, I had

a red motor . . . as a matter of fact, I think it was chapter six something, verses three, four or five, or something where, uh, it was a man, it was a man. On a red horse. And, and, a man on a red horse came out, and uh, and uh, uh, and he was given a knife, and unto him was given the power to kill and destroy. And I actually thought I was this person. And I thought that my red horse was this red Harley Davidson I had. And I wore . . . it was just, you know, it was kind of a symbolic type of thing. And, and, and uh, you know, uh, after the murders I thought the nephew was, was the, was a new devil or something, you know. This, this is pretty bizarre now that I think back on it. I thought he was a new devil and uh, uh. I mean basically I love my sister, there's no question about that. But at times my sister hadn't come through, uh, for me. You know and I was in another one of these manic attacks. And uh, and uh, uh, uh, you know, uh, I was just uh, I was just you know, I mean I was fed up with all this, you know, one day they treat me good and then they tell all these other people that I was a maniac and watch out for me and etcetera and like that. And uh, uh, so I went to them that night to tell them I was all in trouble again, you know, and could they put me up for the night, you know, and they told me to take a hike and uh, so, uh, believing that I had the power to kill, uh, you know, that was that for them. You know. I mean when family turns you out, that's a real blow. You know. But uh, back to the original subject of forgiveness. If I forgive myself, I'm forgiven. You know that's essentially the answer. I'm the captain of my own ship. I run my own ship. Nobody can crawl in my ship unless they get permission. I just *(He nods)* "over there." You know. "I'm forgiven." You know. Ha ha. You know. *(Laughs)* It's as simple as that. You know. You're your own priest, you're your own leader, you're your own captain. You know. You run your own show, a lot of people know that.

MIDDLE FINGER

By Han Ong

The story of five adolescent boys coming of age, Middle Finger *explores issues of "outsiderness," particularly with respect to race and class. While partly an adaptation of* Spring Awakening, *the play is also Han Ong's response to Wedekind's classic. He intended his own play, he says in an* American Theatre *magazine interview, "to find a language suitable to boys—you know, gross and adolescent—and see if the audience is still able to get on their side." Benjamin Lunga is Filipino-American, from a lower-class family; earnest and a good student, he wants to improve his life. When a teacher (called "Dickless" by the boys) accuses him of copying a school essay and then lying about it, Benjamin decides to take revenge with tragic consequences. Here, he tells his friend Jakob how he killed his stepfather—accidentally, but without remorse.*

LUNGA: Do you believe that the dead can come back? [. . .] The dead come back in order to settle unfinished business. [. . .] My stepfather came back tonight. He was sitting at the edge of my bed. I thought I was going to die. Do you know what he wanted? [. . .] I killed him. [. . .] This is how it happened. I mixed Drano in a glass with water. It sizzled the way oil does over a strong fire. Then it stopped. I waited to see what color it would turn. Do you know what came out? Light blue. So light it was almost imperceptible. Like a dim light bulb was shining through it. I wanted to taste it it was so beautiful. But more than that I wanted to give it to Dickless. I wanted him to taste it. A piece of shit! A fucking piece of fucking shit! I never copied a thing in my life! Doesn't he know how hard I worked! In my imagination I was giving him the drink. I was holding it out to him the way you dangle a bone in front of a dog. And his eyes were big, his tongue hanging out like the air was wine.

He's an alcoholic, do you know that? I've seen him sip from a flask he hides inside his briefcase. He took the glass from my hands. And then put it to his mouth. And then nothing. He didn't die. He wasn't dying. He just laughed at me. He kept laughing. Suddenly I realized I was back in our kitchen. I put the glass down into the sink and rushed to my room and I locked the door. I wanted to be as far away from that glass as possible. What was I thinking? Why didn't I just throw it down the drain?! The next thing I remember was footsteps down the stairs. I don't know how much time had gone by. The footsteps were heading towards the kitchen. Suddenly I remembered the glass sitting in the sink. I heard a funny noise and then I rushed down. Just in time to see my stepfather. There was no light on in the kitchen and he must have picked the glass up by mistake. He had it right at his mouth! My glass! With the dim light bulb, which I can now see, was in the exact shape of a skull shining through it. I could have said something. Warned him. But I stood there remembering every single fight he started with my mother, remembering how he made her feel. I stood there just watching him slowly drink down the liquid. And then he dropped the glass and put his hands on his neck like he was choking himself and stuff started coming out of his mouth like the sick rabid dog that he was. But I still didn't go near. I waited a long time till I was sure he was dead. Then I called my mom. [. . .]

And tonight he came back. He was so white. He just sat there at the edge of my bed. Nothing came out of his mouth. Not a word. At first I was scared. But I looked him right in the eye and I kept looking and he realized that I had no remorse. And then he disappeared. He won't be coming back again. I'm sure of it. Don't tell anyone, Jakob.

FURTHER READING

At *American Theatre* magazine/TCG we have been honored to work with the following writers to provide a permanent home for their art. We urge you to further explore the work of these exceptional artists.

This list is compiled alphabetically by author. The *American Theatre* issue information comes first; book publication information, if available, is set last.

JON ROBIN BAITZ
Three Hotels, September 1993; from *Three Hotels: Plays and Monologues*, TCG, New York, 1994.

ERIC BOGOSIAN
Talk Radio, November 1987; from *The Essential Bogosian*, TCG, New York, 1994.

ANTHONY CLARVOE
The Living, December 1993.

STEVEN DIETZ
Lonely Planet, December 1995; published by Dramatists Play Service, Inc., New York, 1994.

RITA DOVE
The Darker Face of the Earth, November 1996; published by Story Line Press, Ashland, OR, 3rd Edition, 2000.

CHRISTOPHER DURANG

The Marriage of Bette and Boo, March 1986; published by Grove/Atlantic, Inc., New York, 1987.

DAVID FELDSHUH

Miss Evers' Boys, November 1990; published by Dramatists Play Service, Inc., New York, 1998.

HORTON FOOTE

The Young Man from Atlanta, September 1995.

ATHOL FUGARD

Playland, March 1993; from *Playland and A Place with the Pigs*, TCG, New York, 1993.

PHILIP KAN GOTANDA

Ballad of Yachiyo, February 1996; published by TCG, New York, 1997.

RICHARD GREENBERG

Three Days of Rain, March 1998; from *Three Days of Rain and Other Plays*, Grove/Atlantic, Inc., New York, 1999.

DAVID HENRY HWANG

M. Butterfly, July 1988; published by Penguin USA, New York, 1994.

MOISÉS KAUFMAN

Gross Indecency: The Three Trials of Oscar Wilde, November 1997; published by Vintage Books, a division of Random House, Inc., 1998.

KEVIN KLING

Lloyd's Prayer, November 1988.

HARRY KONDOLEON

Zero Positive, September 1988; published by Dramatists Play Service, Inc., New York, 1998.

HOWARD KORDER
Search and Destroy, June 1990; published by Grove/Atlantic, Inc., New York, 1992.

TONY KUSHNER
Angels in America, Part One: Millennium Approaches, June 1992; published by TCG, New York, 1992, 1993, 1995.

WARREN LEIGHT
Side Man, December 1998; published by Grove/Atlantic, Inc., New York, 1999.

EDUARDO MACHADO
The Day You'll Love Me (a translation of the play by José Ignacio Cabrujas), September 1989.

DAVID MAMET
Three Sisters (adapted from the play by Anton Chekhov), July 1991; published by Grove/Atlantic, Inc., New York, 1991.

DONALD MARGULIES
Sight Unseen, November 1992; from *Sight Unseen and Other Plays*, TCG, New York, 1995.

HEATHER MCDONALD
An Almost Holy Picture, February 2000.

CHARLES L. MEE
bobrauschenbergamerica, September 2001; available at www.charlesmee.org.

STEPHEN METCALFE
The Incredibly Famous Willy Rivers, January 1986.

MARLANE MEYER
The Chemistry of Change, September 1998.

RICHARD NELSON
Principia Scriptoriae, July 1986; published by Faber and Faber, New York, 1992.

ROBERT O'HARA
Insurrection: Holding History, February 1998; published by TCG, New York, 1999.

HAN ONG
Middle Finger, February 2001.

OYAMO
I Am a Man, November 1993; published by Applause Books, New York, 1995.

SUZAN-LORI PARKS
The America Play, March 1994; from *The America Play and Other Works*, TCG, New York, 1995.

In the Blood, March 2000; from *The Red Letter Plays*, TCG, New York, 2001.

SYBILLE PEARSON
Unfinished Stories, January 1993; published by Dramatists Play Service, Inc., New York, 1998.

REYNOLDS PRICE
August Snow, January 1990; from *New Music*, TCG, New York, 1990.

DAVID RABE
A Question of Mercy, July 1997; published by Grove/Atlantic, Inc., New York, 1998.

JOSÉ RIVERA
Marisol, July 1993; from *Marisol and Other Plays*, TCG, New York, 1997.

MILCHA SANCHEZ-SCOTT
Roosters, September 1987; published by Dramatists Play Service, Inc., New York, 1998.

SAM SHEPARD
Buried Child, September 1996; from *Sam Shepard: Seven Plays*, Bantam Doubleday Dell, a division of Random House, Inc., New York, 1984.

NICKY SILVER
Pterodactyls, February 1994; from *Etiquette and Vitriol: The Food Chain and Other Plays*, TCG, New York, 1996.

OCTAVIO SOLIS
Santos & Santos, November 1995.

STEVE TESICH
The Speed of Darkness, July 1989; published by Samuel French, Inc., New York, 1991.

PAULA VOGEL
The Baltimore Waltz, September 1991; from *The Baltimore Waltz and Other Plays*, TCG, New York, 1996.

NAOMI WALLACE
In the Heart of America, March 1995; from *In the Heart of America and Other Plays*, TCG, New York, 2001.

GEORGE C. WOLFE
The Colored Museum, February 1987; published by Grove/Atlantic, Inc., New York, 1988.

The following list provides contact information regarding performance rights to the works included in this volume:

Jon Robin Baitz c/o Creative Artists Agency, 767 Fifth Ave., NY, NY 10153; Eric Bogosian c/o Creative Artists Agency, 767 Fifth Ave., NY, NY 10153; Anthony Clarvoe c/o Writers and Artists Agency, 19 W. 44th St., Suite 1000, NY, NY 10036; Steven Dietz c/o International Creative Management, 40 W. 57th St., NY, NY 10019; Rita Dove c/o Story Line Press, Three Oaks Farm, Box 1240, Ashland, OR 97520-0055; Christopher Durang c/o Helen Merrill, Ltd., 295 Lafayette St., Suite 915, NY, NY 10012; David Feldshuh c/o Helen Merrill, Ltd., 295 Lafayette St., Suite 915, NY, NY 10012; Horton Foote c/o The Barbara Hogenson Agency, 165 West End Ave., Suite 19C, NY, NY 10023; Athol Fugard c/o William Morris Agency, 1325 Ave. of the Americas, NY, NY 10019; Philip Kan Gotanda c/o Helen Merrill, Ltd., 295 Lafayette St., Suite 915, NY, NY 10012; Richard Greenberg c/o Creative Artists Agency, 767 Fifth Ave., NY, NY 10153; David Henry Hwang c/o Writers and Artists Agency, 19 W. 44th St., Suite 1000, NY, NY 10036; Moisés Kaufman c/o Joyce Ketay Agency, 630 Ninth Ave., Suite 706, NY, NY 10036; Kevin Kling c/o Susan Schulman, A Literary Agency, 454 W. 44th St., NY, NY 10036; Harry Kondoleon c/o William Morris Agency, 1325 Ave. of the Americas, NY, NY 10019; Howard Korder c/o Abrams Artists Agency, 275 Seventh Ave., 26th Floor, NY, NY 10001; Tony Kushner c/o Joyce Ketay Agency, 630 Ninth Ave., Suite 706, NY, NY 10036; Warren Leight c/o Creative Artists Agency, 767 Fifth

Ave., NY, NY 10153; Eduardo Machado c/o Barbara Ligeti, 910 West End Ave., #6F, NY, NY 10025; David Mamet c/o Rosenstone/Wender, 38 E. 29th St., 10th Floor, NY, NY 10016; Donald Margulies c/o Rosenstone/Wender, 38 E. 29th St., 10th Floor, NY, NY 10016; Heather McDonald c/o Peregrine Whittlesey Agency, 345 E. 80th St., Suite 31F, NY, NY 10021; Charles L. Mee c/o International Creative Management, 40 W. 57th St., NY, NY 10019; Stephen Metcalfe c/o TCG; Marlane Meyer c/o The Gersh Agency, 41 Madison Ave., NY, NY 10010; Richard Nelson c/o The Gersh Agency, 41 Madison Ave., NY, NY 10010; Robert O'Hara c/o Rosenstone/Wender, 38 E. 29th St., 10th Floor, NY, NY 10016; Han Ong c/o International Creative Management, 40 W. 57th St., NY, NY 10019; OyamO c/o Berman, Boals and Flynn, 208 W. 30th St., Suite 401, NY, NY 10001; Suzan-Lori Parks c/o Creative Artists Agency, 767 Fifth Ave., NY, NY 10153; Sybille Pearson c/o Joyce Ketay Agency, 630 Ninth Ave., Suite 706, NY, NY 10036; Reynolds Price c/o William Morris Agency, 1325 Ave. of the Americas, NY, NY 10019; David Rabe c/o Joyce Ketay Agency, 630 Ninth Ave., Suite 706, NY, NY 10036; José Rivera c/o Joyce Ketay Agency, 630 Ninth Ave., Suite 706, NY, NY 10036; Milcha Sanchez-Scott c/o William Morris Agency, 1325 Ave. of the Americas, NY, NY 10019; Sam Shepard c/o Berman, Boals and Flynn, 208 W. 30th St., Suite 401, NY, NY 10001; Nicky Silver c/o Creative Artists Agency, 767 Fifth Ave., NY, NY 10153; Octavio Solis c/o TCG; Steve Tesich c/o International Creative Management, 40 W. 57th St., NY, NY 10019; Paula Vogel c/o The Gersh Agency, 41 Madison Ave., NY, NY 10010; Naomi Wallace c/o Joyce Ketay Agency, 630 Ninth Ave., Suite 706, NY, NY 10036; George C. Wolfe c/o Loeb & Loeb, 345 Park Ave., 18th Floor, NY, NY 10154.

STEPHANIE COEN is the director of communications at Seattle's Intiman Theatre. Previously, she was director of publications for The Joseph Papp Public Theater/New York Shakespeare Festival under the artistic leadership of George C. Wolfe. A former managing editor of *American Theatre* magazine, she was on staff at Theatre Communications Group for seven years and wrote TCG's 2000 report on the state of the American theatre, "The Field and Its Challenges."